TOXIC CLIENT

Knowing and Avoiding the Problem Customer

By Garrett Sutton

Published by
Success DNA, Inc.
2248 Meridian Boulevard, Suite H.
Minden, Nevada 89423

Printed in the United States of America

First Edition: 2016

ISBN: 978-1-944194-03-1

I would like to acknowledge the input and valuable assistance of Frank Troppe, Kenji Sax, Cindie Geddes, Mark Goodman, Elizabeth Ryan, Tom Wheelwright, Jessica Santina and Lyn Millard. Thanks to all of you for thoughts, stories and insights.

Books by Garrett Sutton

Start Your Own Corporation
Run Your Own Corporation
The ABCs of Getting Out of Debt
Writing Winning Business Plans
Buying & Selling a Business
Loopholes of Real Estate
How to Use Limited Liability Companies and Limited Partnerships
Finance Your Own Business

CONTENTS

Foreword

Your phone rings and you immediately recognize the caller ID. You think: "If this guy is calling me one more time with grief, I am going to reach through the phone, grab him by the throat and squeeze until his eyeballs pop out!"

Sound familiar? If you are in any kind of business, I am sure you can relate to this. It's that one client who will not go away. The one who seems to just want to pull the chain of your team and staff, complaining and demanding about either the most mundane things or the most outrageous requests.

There are even some who seem to "know" how to implant enough truth into their demands that you actually begin to feel like you did something wrong! Now do you know what I mean?

For over 25 years, I have coached, trained and supported thousands of entrepreneurs all over the world. I know as an entrepreneur you want to serve the world, reach as many people as you can, provide an amazing product and service and make a lot of money doing it. Yet in that quest to reach the world, it turns out that you end up reaching some who you would rather not. Ones that can never be satisfied, ones that stress your entire team, or ones that just want you to know they are always around.

Unfortunately, it comes with the territory.

Eighty percent of your good business comes from twenty percent of your clients. And eighty percent of your problems, stress and angst come from another twenty percent. But that is only part of the problem.

Just as problematic is that you could be getting rave reviews from most of your customers, kicking butt all over the market and feeling great about you and your team. But when that one Toxic Client activates their spell on you or your team, all your focus is on that one customer.

It's our natural instinct to focus on the problems. We want them fixed. Yet is it actually healthy to fixate 80% of your energy on those handfuls of thorny issues and clients? Or is it better to take your good energies, intentions and strengths and drive the growth and prosperity of your business?

What if you could spend most of your day growing your business rather than running in circles dealing with problems that are...well...really not that big of a problem?

This book, *Toxic Client* by my friend Garrett Sutton, is better therapy for you than a team of psychologists. It will free your mind, lift the vague guilt and allow you to focus on your strengths rather than being distracted by the overly "squeaky wheels." In a market that looks more like a blizzard, the Toxic Client succeeds in making their presence known. They give us decent feedback from time to time, but if they win the focus of your attention, they have crippled you.

You must have a commitment to excellence. Let it be your strength and not the Achilles Heel that others can prey upon. You must learn to avoid and dismiss the Toxic Client. This book will show you how.

Be awesome.

Blair Singer

Global Training Entrepreneur and Rich Dad Advisor,

Bestselling author of *SalesDogs*,

Team Code of Honor and

Little Voice Mastery

Introduction:

Who is a Toxic Client?

As an entrepreneur and business owner you are an optimist. You see the positives and plan for the successes.

You must also be a realist. You must plan for the inevitable challenges associated with running a business. You must be aware of all the dark corners. And when it comes to darkness, one of the biggest challenges you will face is the Toxic Client.

The word 'toxic' is not a happy one. Any word synonymous with poison, death and pestilence represents something very serious to avoid. Our natural preferences, our multi-millennial honed instincts, are geared toward staying away from toxicity. Evolution has taught us some very powerful lessons.

But evolution has failed to weed out the toxic people among us, from our places of work and our business relationships. Indeed, with the spread of drug usage and onset of Entitlementia described in Chapters Seven and Eight, the numbers of Toxic Clients have increased. Toxic personalities, from the entitled and narcissist to the bully and manipulator, inhabit our common space. You all know that they are out there.

A Toxic Client is a person that sets you back in a significant way. More than a mere nuisance, they are a distinct detriment to you, your team and your company's morale. In terms of time, money and effort the Toxic Client is a drain on resources and a drag on revenue. The damage wrought by a Toxic Client can be severe. These are not people who simply bother us. These are people capable of poisoning and contaminating entire organizations.

Their toxicity can be a cancer. If you allow it.

This book is about knowing and avoiding the Toxic Client. Again, you know that they are out there. If you have been in business for any length of time you have probably knowingly dealt with at least one of them. If you are to succeed in business over the long term you must know how to identify and dismiss them.

Healthy organizations survive best when not beset by toxins in the form of everyday clients. Business is tough enough with taxation, regulations, competition, price pressures and all the employee issues. To further be challenged by those you are just trying to do business with may seem inconsequential when compared to the aforementioned business risks. But the individual Toxic Client, or a set of policies which encourages multiple Toxic Clients, can more frequently and quickly shut down a business than a government audit or employee harassment claim. Owner beware.

I have sat in a great chair for viewing the Toxic Client. First, as a lawyer assisting people with corporate and asset protection strategies, I have had a few Toxic Clients over the years. Every lawyer does. The old joke that the best law practice is one without clients is based on the experience every lawyer has in their encounters with Toxic Clients.

Secondly, my view has been enriched by dealing with a very large number of entrepreneurs and investors. My practice focuses on structuring and forming corporations and LLCs.

Typically, I have a conversation about how best to structure and protect their business and investments and then the paralegals do the formations. Over the years have I consulted with a large number of clients. This has been enjoyable for a number of reasons, including getting to know people from all walks and businesses from around the world. I like the positive energy of entrepreneurs and investors.

In my conversations with these many people I frequently hear about their legal challenges. I have learned that the Toxic Client is a frequent nemesis to all. One of the reasons for corporations, LLCs and asset protection is to prevent Toxic Clients from suing to get at all of your personal assets. (This issue is a whole other book I have written entitled *Start Your Own Corporation*.) The stories I have heard, some of which are in this book under appropriate disguise, reflect the many shapes and varieties of Toxic Clients. And from these stories I have learned how entrepreneurs and others successfully identify and dismiss such flawed customers.

To succeed in business you must learn these strategies too. It helps to learn them right from the start.

Toxic Clients appear early. In that first flush of life as business owners, we often say "yes" to anyone who wants to hire us. We think the most important thing is establishing a client base. Beggars can't be choosers, right? As long as we're getting hired, that's a good thing, and it's all that matters.

But after a while, we learn an important truth: Not every client is a good client. In fact, some of them are truly toxic— they contaminate our business environment and breed negativity about the work, they infect employees by lowering their morale, they exhaust and debilitate our energy reserves, and they drain our coffers.

Like pollution or a disease, Toxic Clients are destructive to your business and your health. And chances are you've worked with at least one.

Perhaps you're already thinking about a client or two who might fit this category. Have you ever had a client who complained incessantly, either about your work or about the work others have done which you now have to "fix"? Were you ever nickel-and-dimed over your "excessively high" fees? Did a client ever conveniently stop receiving your emails or responding to your inquiries once it was time for you to be paid? Has a client ever made you feel both miserable and exhausted? Did you ever feel like you were going crazy because a client kept asking you to do one thing and then, the next day, asking you to do the opposite? Have you ever had a client whose only physical activity is jumping to conclusions, all of which they exercise against you?

If any of these situations sound familiar, or if they remind you of other clients that have driven you nuts, you've had a Toxic Client.

The Customer is Always Right?

Really? The Customer Is Always Right?

Are they right when they won't pay? Are they right when they return merchandise they've already heavily used? Are they right when they scream and show absolutely no gratitude for your assistance?

Of course not. Despite the time worn adage, the customer is most certainly not always right.

With a good customer you are free to honor the adage. With a Toxic Client you must sometimes nullify it. Sometimes the better course is to just say no. As in 'yes' you are the customer but 'no' you are not right. We will deal with this issue further in Chapter Four on Freeloaders.

Taking on a Toxic Client is not a step forward for you. It is a step backward. You will expend twice the effort you should as you chase your tail trying to please this client. And guess what? You never will. You'll earn half of what your time and energy are worth (if, in fact, you earn any money at all from your Toxic Client). Meanwhile, you'll shortchange the valuable clients who are worth your time.

If your business is going to succeed you must learn to recognize Toxic Clients before it's too late. You must understand why such clients are toxic, learn how to extract yourself from a current Toxic Client and, ultimately, avoid working with a Toxic Client ever again.

This book is designed to share these lessons with you. In the following pages, I've included stories from a wide range of business owners who have dealt with Toxic Clients—including myself. You'll see that no industry is immune to difficult clients who complain, constantly change their minds, yell at you or others, make unreasonable demands, second-guess you, miss appointments, refuse to listen, or won't pay up. And through these stories, you'll learn to recognize the signs of a Toxic Client right from the get-go. By doing so you won't later have to give them the heave-ho. You won't take them in the first place, to the benefit of your staff, your company's future and your own sanity.

Chapter One:

Listen

"Hearing is one of the body's five senses. But listening is an art."
~ Frank Tyger

If you're like me, the first fifty times or so that your parents tried to impart some life lesson, you either flat-out ignored it or filed it away in the back of your brain as you rolled your eyes and said, "Yeah, whatever." It's only when you eventually learned that lesson the hard way that you acknowledged their wisdom, and that little voice in your head piped up with, "Oh, so that's what they meant!"

Here I'm speaking from experience. My father was a district attorney, in private practice and eventually an Alameda County Superior Court Judge based in Oakland, California. As I was getting started as an attorney, he repeatedly told me that the most valuable legal strategy was knowing which clients not to take.

But as a newly minted lawyer, I was keen on taking whatever walked in the door. And I thought there were a number of good reasons to do so: I needed the experience, I needed the work, and I was, at some level, kind of flattered that someone wanted me as their lawyer.

So when William Napoli walked in the door with a lease dispute, I was all ears. Unfortunately, I didn't use my own ears as much as I should have.

William told me that his landlord had failed to make the necessary tenant improvements on his restaurant space. Because of this, William had been unable to continue operating his Italian restaurant—the restaurant that had been his lifelong goal and dream to open in the first place. He was forced to close the restaurant shortly thereafter, and the landlord was now suing William for the tenant improvements, back rent and other damages.

After listening to William and quickly reviewing the documents, I said I would need a $1,000 retainer against my then-hourly rate of $125. William said he could pay me $500 right away and would come up with the remaining $500 at the end of the week. He said he would pay his legal bill promptly.

Taking him at his word, I answered the landlord's complaint as William's attorney, thus making an appearance in the case.

In the next few months, I learned several important lessons. First, although William had promised he would pay the rest of the retainer and his legal bills, he did no such thing. In fact, I soon discovered that William had a history of not paying his bills.

I also learned that once you make an appearance in a case, a judge doesn't have to let you out. When it became clear that my client wouldn't pay for my services, I made a motion to the court asking for permission to withdraw myself as William's attorney. Of course, preparing, filing, and arguing that motion constituted even more (unpaid) time for me.

Many judges routinely grant these motions. Many were in private practice themselves and had faced the same issues with some of their clients. But not every judge will grant a motion to withdraw. And in this case, my judge denied my motion. (I've always thought that the judge – like my dad – wanted to teach me a lesson.) As a result, I had to defend William, whether I got paid or not. And so I fulfilled my obligation and defended William to the best of my ability.

And for my efforts, I received only a meager $500, for all of it.

It was the best experience I could have ever had, really. Because that experience taught me that I really need to listen to what a client is saying. In fact, I need to listen to what's between the lines of what the client is saying, too. William had actually told me everything I needed to know. Through what he'd said, and what he had conveniently left out, he had actually announced that he was a Toxic Client. I just hadn't been paying attention, because I was so focused on getting a new client.

William had claimed that the landlord had failed to make the necessary improvements to his restaurant space. But if that was the case, why had he even opened the business in the first place? I didn't ask that question then, but I would now. William said he had to close the restaurant shortly after opening it. Was it really because of the lack of improvements? Or could it have been his food? Or the fact that he didn't pay his bills?

Asking for the client retainer was another listening opportunity.

When William balked at my retainer and indicated that he didn't have the money, he was giving me a signal that he was only interested in what I could do for him, not in the value of my services. Perhaps he knew I had only recently gone into practice and thought he'd take advantage of my inexperience. Otherwise, he never would have come to an attorney's office unprepared to pay for services.

You need to listen to how the client reacts to and deals with such a request. If he or she values your services and respects the fact that you can't work for free, you will hear quite a different response than the one offered by a client, like William, who only wants to milk your skills because he desperately needs your help at that moment.

There are more than a few clients out there who believe that all lawyers are overpaid, and thus can afford to take a case at a reduced rate. And it's not just attorneys that deal with it. This attitude prevails in all industries, among all professionals. Whether you're a doctor, an engineer, a plumber, a hairstylist, a designer, or a house cleaner, you're going to encounter clients who think you can absorb the loss of taking them on as a client, that you can afford to do the work for what they're willing to pay, and, in some cases, that you're lucky to get the work in the first place.

These types of clients not only will not pay you, but they will also create so many problems for you that they become what I call "tar babies"—sticky, messy bundles of problems from which it's extremely difficult to extricate yourself. (We will deal with tar babies in Chapter Nine).

But if you are to succeed, the Toxic Client must be avoided. So listen carefully, because the Toxic Client might just announce himself to you.

Lesson #1: If you listen well, the Toxic Client will tell you everything you need to know.

Case No. 1: The Personal Trainer

Jeff Kerry seemed like he would be an ideal client for personal trainer Matthew Martinez. As chief officer of his family's large engineering company, Kerry was well-heeled and could easily afford Martinez's hourly rate. And since the wealthy talk to the wealthy, Martinez thought Kerry could prove to be a valuable source of referrals.

Kerry had been referred to Martinez, who was a regular trainer at the upscale tennis and health club where Kerry's family had a membership. Kerry had asked the clerks at the desk for a male trainer, and the clerks had offered Martinez's name. Martinez just happened to have an opening in his schedule, and he was one of the club's most experienced trainers. Martinez had been training himself for 16 years, and he had been a personal trainer for five years, with certification from the International Sports Science Association.

Kerry contacted Martinez and immediately booked two one-hour sessions per week, on Mondays and Wednesdays. Right from the start, he proved to be a challenge and was full of complaints.

"He was awfully picky about the temperature in the gym," Martinez says. "It was either too warm and stuffy, or too cold. I constantly had to open the door or adjust the thermostat."

Then there was the hour of his appointment, which seemed to always be inconvenient. "He didn't want to stay in his spot," Martinez remembers. "He'd show up late, and say, 'Well, I need a later spot.' I'd try to schedule him later, and then he'd say, 'I want an early spot now.'"

Martinez got to talking with another client, one who knew Kerry personally. This client told Martinez that Kerry had a reputation for chiseling construction contractors on engineering jobs. He'd haggle over their invoices and never pay in full.

But this didn't add up for Martinez. Kerry kept his family's account current at the health club. The fifty-something business executive also seemed dedicated during his workouts. He wanted to build muscle, lose weight, and increase his flexibility, since Kerry was, as Martinez assessed, "stiff as a board."

"The workouts weren't bad," Martinez recalls. "I could really hammer him. He had a lot of pride and didn't want to look weak. He wanted to be pushed. Push-ups, sit-ups, bench press, squats, lots of stretches. Every once in a while we'd talk about his business, the engineering projects and stuff like that. But he was not a man of a whole lot of words. He came in, did is thing, complained, and left."

Then, one day after six months of twice-a-week workouts, Kerry was a no-show. Martinez stood around waiting at the appointed hour.

There had been no advance phone call from Kerry to cancel or reschedule, nor was there a follow-up call explaining why he'd missed. Martinez called Kerry's cell phone, but only got the voicemail. Martinez left a message, but did not hear back.

At the next scheduled workout session, Kerry was absent again.

Martinez spent another hour waiting in vain—an hour he could have filled with a different client. Martinez felt like he was in limbo. Should he scratch Kerry's name from the tight schedule and book another client in that time slot? Surely, Kerry would make good on the missed appointments, Martinez thought. After all, Kerry was an important business man, one who valued the training and understood what it meant to make appointments.

The following week brought two more missed sessions. Martinez saw Kerry's teenaged daughter working out at the club.

"I asked her what had happened to her father," Martinez says. "She said he was out of the country on a trip to the Far East."

Martinez left another voice message for Kerry, this time saying that the club would be charging him for the missed appointments.

Martinez turned in the usual slip at the club desk so that the family's account would be billed.

It was Kerry's wife who responded to the voice message.

Evidently, she'd reviewed her husband's missed calls in preparation for his return. She was not pleased that they had been billed for the no-shows. She called up the club and demanded that her husband not be charged for the missed sessions. The clerk left a message for Martinez to call her.

"I'm not paying for this bill," she told Martinez over the phone, in a superior, snobbish tone.

Martinez protested: "He didn't tell me he'd be gone, and I was there. You're paying me for my time."

Kerry's wife did not raise her voice. But she did not change her position, either. "I'm not going to pay for the time," she said, smugly.

Martinez was flustered. It's standard practice for personal trainers—and for professionals in other fields that set appointments with clients, such as dance instructors, massage therapists and hair-dressers—to bill clients who fail to give a minimum 24-hour notice of a cancellation.

"I fill my hours," Martinez says, "and if somebody flakes and has already bought my time, that's how it works."

Martinez explained this to Kerry's wife, but it was to no avail. Her mind was set. Martinez was not paid for the no-shows.

The long-term listening strategy involves hearing and evaluating what the client says throughout the term of the relationship. In the case of the personal trainer, Jeff Kerry was constantly complaining about everything, including the hour of his appointment. A client who constantly wants to shift his time to fit his ever-shifting schedule is ignorant of the fact that personal trainers need to assign people to fairly fixed schedules in order to maximize their earning potential. The client who is unwilling to stand in the shoes of the provider and appreciate their business position is the client who must be told the rules early on.

When the trainer, Matthew Martinez, kept hearing about schedule changes, he needed to interpret and evaluate what was being said.

Essentially, Jeff Kerry's actions revealed that he did not care about Martinez's business model. If Martinez had given Kerry's words a proper evaluation, he would have developed a written policy about missed appointments. If Martinez had addressed the issue early on, in anticipation of the inevitable problem, he would have had a client who called ahead to cancel, out of consideration for his time, or who would at least have paid him for the missed appointments. Instead, he had a client who took advantage of his time and valued it even less.

Case No. 2: The CPA

Victor Lee was a CPA in Seattle. He had a good practice handling the bookkeeping and tax work for a number of businesses and individuals.

One day, John Yang came into the office looking for a new CPA. He indicated that his last CPA had improperly filed a tax return, which had caused him problems with the IRS. As the initial client consultation went on, Yang also complained about two other previous accounting professionals he had used. He said that they didn't know what they were doing.

Lee liked to bring in new clients to the firm. As some of his elderly clients passed on, he always felt the need to attract new accounts so his billings would be equal to or higher than those of the previous year. He listened to Yang's explanation of his background without focusing on the caustic comments expressing dissatisfaction with all his previous accountants.

Lee agreed to take on Yang's work. He filed an amended tax return for Yang, sent out a bill, and did not hear from or receive payments from Yang.

Three years later, Yang called Lee in a panic. The IRS had put a lien on his bank account. Yang was furious that Lee had allowed this to happen. Initially, Lee drew a blank. He hadn't heard from Yang for a few years and couldn't recall the file. He asked if he could call Yang back, and that's when Yang made another disparaging comment about accountants.

Now he remembered Yang.

If Victor Lee had listened carefully to John Yang, he would have heard the signs of a Toxic Client. He would have heard that John Yang has financial trouble—why else would he repeatedly have problems with the IRS? He would have heard John Yang say all his previous CPAs didn't know what they were doing – a sure sign of future trouble for you.

Listening is a key technique for dealing with or avoiding Toxic Clients like Yang. Too often, business owners see listening as a two-step process:

1. Listen to what is said.
2. Respond to what is said.

But this doesn't account for your processing of the information you take in when listening. Rather, you should consider engaging in active listening, which is a four-step process:

1. Listen to what is said.
2. Interpret what is said.
3. Evaluate what is said.
4. Respond to what is said.

As you listen to the client, you need to interpret and evaluate what is being said. Actually, you unconsciously do this anyway. But by recognizing and focusing on these steps, and making them a priority, you will be much better at identifying the true natures of your potential clients.

When you force yourself to actively interpret information as it's given to you, rather than passively taking in the information as it's presented, you're assigning it meaning. If you're not sure that you have correctly interpreted what's been said, ask questions until you can make a clear interpretation.

When you make an evaluation, you weigh the information and decide how to apply it. The task is to keep listening (and to ask questions to further your listening) until you have enough information to make the correct decision.

The active listening process is both a short-term and long-term strategy for avoiding the Toxic Client. In Victor Lee's case, the client made his dislike of accounting professionals known in the initial interview. As longtime professionals know, when someone complains about the mistreatment he's received from others in your field, chances are good that he'll be complaining about you next.

Active listening requires singular focus. Too many of us are trying to do too many things at once—checking email, looking at notes, responding to texts and thinking of what next to say. But if you're going to avoid a Toxic Client, you can't be distracted.

A part of listening and evaluating is paying attention to those non-verbal signals that clients give us. You can 'hear' what people say in part by what their body language and tone of voice indicate. Learn to interpret the various non-verbal cues to your advantage.

Signs of impatience or annoyance include finger tapping, shifting of weight from one foot to another, abrupt or rapid speech, or a rise in voice volume or pitch. Clients shouldn't display anger or impatience in an initial consultation. If one does, there's a high likelihood that you're interacting with a potentially Toxic Client. Their next bout of anger may be directed at you.

As well, clients shouldn't go on and on with elaborate tales of woe. Many want you to be an enabler of their victimhood. You probably won't be able to help this person and they will drag you down even if you somehow can. (Again, more on tar babies in Chapter Nine). Listen carefully, and evaluate even more carefully.

Finally, here's another benefit of active listening: You'll not only be able to weed out Toxic Clients, but you'll also probably learn more about the clients you want to keep, and develop stronger relationships with them as a result.

Of course, listening has played a big part in the creation of this book. I have listened to the experiences of a number of friends and clients. I have come to realize in general terms and through a thoroughly non- scientific sampling that:

95% have encountered Toxic Clients.

80% have dealt with non-paying clients.

50% have been stiffed (never paid) by a client.

40% regularly deal with clients who take longer than
     90 days to pay.

In listening to these stories and learning of the common experiences shared by all business owners it becomes abundantly clear: The Customer Is Not Always Right.

Chapter Two:

Angry

"Anger is really disappointed hope."
~ Erica Jong

"It is the growling man who lives a dog's life."
~ Coleman Cox

If you have been in business for any length of time, you have dealt with an angry client. It may be due to personal issues, the client's mental health, a full moon, or one of a hundred other reasons. But the cold fact of the matter is that when you deal with the public, some of those people are going to be angry.

Is it up to you to solve the angry client's problem or meet his or her needs? Maybe not. Are all angry clients toxic? Not necessarily. They may be justified in their anger, and by employing some of the strategies we will discuss here, you can work toward building a more productive relationship.

But some angry people are displaying the first indications of toxicity. And once you learn how to recognize that, you can send them on their way.

Case No. 3: The Dermatologist

The shrill woman on the other end of the telephone line was angry and abusive. She was enraged about not being able to book an appointment at the dermatologist's office.

Dr. Sarah Adams shared her practice with three other dermatologists. Their typical client was a woman between the ages of 30 and 50 who was seeking cosmetic services such as Botox and collagen treatments, facials, chemical peels, and laser hair removal. These clients came in because they wanted to look younger, healthier and more attractive.

Dr. Adams' husband, Kenny Adams, helped manage the office. So on this day, when the receptionist finally couldn't take any more screaming from the angry woman on the phone, she put the woman on hold and asked Kenny to deal with the caller who was demanding to be seen because she had a wart, and wouldn't accept that the office was booked two months in advance.

Adams picked up the call and calmly explained to the angry woman that he was the office manager and that an appointment could only be made when there was an opening. Unfortunately, he said, the doctors in this office were in high demand. He encouraged her to call around to see if another dermatologist could see her sooner.

"No, I want to see Dr. Adams!" she screamed. Then she began insulting Kenny, calling him "ridiculous," "stubborn," and "unprofessional."

Kenny managed to control his temper, realizing that directing anger back at her would certainly not help the situation. But his calm demeanor only resulted in further torrents of insults.

After several minutes of listening calmly to the woman, Kenny employed a firm tone and said, "Ma'am, I can't help you if you yell and scream at me or call me abusive names. We don't book appointments for people who act in an angry or abusive manner."

"Yes, sir!" said the woman, sarcastically.

"We treat our patients with respect, and we expect the same thing in return," Kenny continued.

"Yes, sir!" she repeated.

It was at this point that Kenny realized this was a lost cause. She was a Toxic Client who behaved irrationally. He decided not to proceed with helping her. "If you can't schedule an appointment with another doctor, call us back," Kenny told her. "But this doesn't sound like an emergency, so we can only give you the next available opening."

At this, the woman hung up. Kenny never heard from her again.

The previous story illustrates an important first step for dealing with an angry client: Listen calmly.

As tempting as it might be to avoid angry clients ("Maybe if I ignore it or walk away, the client will cool off") it is not a useful business strategy. The client may cool off momentarily, but it doesn't eliminate the problem. It only postpones it. And if he or she doesn't cool off, you risk that client filing complaints or spreading bad word-of-mouth. While positive word-of-mouth is great for business, negative word-of-mouth gets spread at a far greater rate, and is downright damaging to your company. You want to avoid it, but sometimes with a Toxic Client – you just can't.

Was Kenny Adams' caller justified in her anger? No. Was Kenny's response, to calmly listen, the right one? Absolutely.

The soundest business advice is to deal with angry clients right away, to do what you can to rectify the situation before you potentially lose business. Of course, Kenny's angry caller could very well go disparage the dermatology practice to all her friends. There's nothing he can do about that. But he can rest easy in the knowledge that he did what he could to address and solve the problem. That's all any of us can do.

The first step is empathy. Often, the biggest part of anger is frustration at not being heard or understood. Stand in their shoes for a moment. If appropriate, say that you understand why they are upset and that you would be upset too in such a situation. Listen, maintain eye contact, and without any other distraction be attentive to their personal matter.

Empathy has a way of defusing anger. At this point, a reasonable person would think, "OK, good, at least someone gets how important this is to me." If the person is still unreasonable, that's a whole other issue.

When people acknowledge that they've made mistakes and accept responsibility, others' estimation of them tends to go up. We respect such actions. If a mistake has been made, simply saying, "I'm sorry" can go a long way toward impressing the client and eliminating some of that anger that's being directed at you. If no mistake has been made the empathetic statement "I understand" can be very helpful.

Let the client get it all out. Don't be critical of a person's anger or try to contain it, and don't interrupt. Venting allows people to deflate the problem themselves. The client may come to realize they've blown it all out of proportion, and they will accept any resolution you offer. After venting the pent up anger will dissipate. So don't discourage it or cut it off. Let the balloon of anger fully deflate.

Once you've come to this point of the conversation, you can begin to deal with the issue. The first question you should ask is "What would you like me to do to help you?" It's a simple question that is often overlooked, but it gets to the heart of problem-solving. It's possible that the client doesn't know what he or she wants you to do. Take this opportunity to clarify what's really being requested and begin to solve the problem.

Proceed calmly. Be the rational one. Explain the alternatives that are available to you that get closest to meeting the client's needs. Ask questions. For instance, Kenny Adams might ask, "Can I take your number and call you if we have a cancellation?", "I'm interested in knowing why you aren't happy with any of our other doctors; how can I resolve that for you?", or "Are you sure I can't refer you to another great doctor with greater availability?"

Here's a situation that illustrates how effective this simple technique can be.

Case No. 4: The Salesperson

John Minden was Ellen Bay's best customer. He accounted for almost 30 percent of her yearly sales, and she always took steps to maintain an open and positive relationship with him. When Minden called her with a big order, she dropped everything and went directly to his office. She promised a three-week turnaround and promptly turned in the order to her production department.

Three weeks later, Bay dropped in to make sure all was well with her client. It was at that point that Bay first learned what her production department had already told Minden: The model he had ordered was no longer available.

Minden was livid. Bay had never seen such anger in her client. But because he was a client that mattered to her, Bay used all her skills to see the argument through with John.

First, she dealt with his anger in the only way possible, which was understanding that she simply couldn't control another person's anger, so it wasn't wise even to try. She was cautious not to be critical of it or try to contain it. Instead, she allowed Minden's anger to vent.

As he calmed down, Bay made it clear that she empathized with him. She used phrases such as, "I understand how you feel," and "I'd be angry if the same thing happened to me."

Bay then decided that the anger would not affect the relationship. This was a crucial step; instead of interpreting Minden's anger as a sign of his toxicity, she determined that he was a client worth keeping. She told him, "Your business is important to me. I appreciate your candor in this situation. I will work even harder to make this relationship work and resolve this problem."

Eventually, John Minden calmed down and, seeing Bay's willingness to work with her, forgave the mistake and allowed her to rectify the situation with a credit toward the next order.

As you can see from this example, simply meeting the client halfway with empathy helps to defuse the situation, and at this point you can begin to work on solving any problems and strengthening the relationship. Remember, you won't get to this step until after the client has expressed his or her anger.

The venting and purging must occur before the rebuilding begins, or else you'll be building on a bitter foundation doomed to collapse. People have a way of hanging onto old grudges if they aren't dealt with. And psychologists will tell you that when people survive an emotionally challenging event together, it often leads to a lasting bond between them. Like a disaster movie, where the male and female leads can't stand each other at the start, after all the explosions and near-death experiences you know they will get together at the end.

See yourself through the challenge. As in Ellen Bay's case, she and John Minden were able to forge an even stronger relationship.

But while Bay was able to rescue, rebuild, and even strengthen her relationship with her best customer, Kenny Adams at the dermatology office had no desire to do the same with his angry caller. The lady on the phone made unreasonable demands and hurled insults that shut communication down. She was toxic from the start. Unlike John Minden's mishandled order, which was a justifiable reason to be angry, Adams' caller had no reason to be upset. The dermatologists hadn't even rendered a service for her yet, and it's very common for dermatology offices to be booked out several weeks. Her reaction was out of proportion, misplaced, and irrational—it was toxic.

Lesson #2: Sometimes anger is justified and worth addressing, and sometimes it's not. Learn to tell the difference.

Case No. 5: The Financial Planner

Financial planner Gerald Westerbrook's new client was George Stinson, a prominent criminal-defense lawyer. Stinson was aggressive and accustomed to getting his way. He wore $2,000 suits and drove a flashy black Mercedes. He represented clients accused of drug dealing or other crimes who were able to pay his sizable retainer in cash. Stinson always made sure to be paid up front. He liked money, and his lifestyle.

One thing he didn't like was the performance of his brokerage account, which was losing money in the stock market. So Stinson contacted Westerbrook about transferring the account to Westerbrook's firm.

Westerbrook was resistant. His cardinal rule in accepting new clients was, "Never clean up another broker's mess." He reasoned that doing so meant he was always playing catch-up, just to get returns back to where they should have been. It was a losing game.

But Stinson, as we know, was persuasive. He knew how to argue to advance his point of view. It was his job to be this way. It took a lot of convincing, but Westerbrook finally agreed to have the $120,000 account transferred.

At first, the move proved successful. Westerbrook held real estate and insurance licenses as well as many registrations to trade different classes of securities, and he was a certified estate advisor. He specialized in portfolio management, retirement accounts, and technology stocks. His typical clients were affluent people in their fifties and sixties. He wrote up a comprehensive retirement plan for Stinson, who also owned real estate. Westerbrook explained the plan thoroughly to his new client.

Stinson agreed to the plan and transferred a total of $120,000 to Westerbrook. Over the next 24 months, the account performed well, earning returns that were higher than the overall market performance. Stinson seemed pleased, and Westerbrook was satisfied, too. The two began to enjoy a good client-advisor relationship.

It was about a year later that this began to change. Stinson phoned Westerbrook sounding different from usual—hostile and on the attack.

"I just saw my quarterly statement," the lawyer said angrily, "and I'm extremely upset that I'm losing money!"

Westerbrook was both surprised and taken back. "Excuse me," he said firmly, "don't use that tone with me. Didn't you see my email from two weeks ago that said you're making 13 percent average per year?"

"Don't get smart with me," responded Stinson, his voice rising. "I'm not getting smart with you," Westerbrook said evenly. "Those are the facts."

The facts, Westerbrook continued, were that Stinson's account had actually made strong gains. Westerbrook quickly punched buttons on a calculator. "Your account has earned approximately $50,000."

"That's bull!" Stinson shouted into the phone. "I'm looking at the quarterly statement right here! I've got the balance right here in front of me! I am way down on this thing."

Westerbrook was exasperated and replied, "You're still not back to your original investment because of the losses the other broker created for you when I inherited the account. You've made gains, but it's on a smaller amount. That has nothing to do with me."

To which Stinson yelled, "Screw you!" and slammed down the phone.

This story illustrates another important point about angry clients: Sometimes they aren't even angry at you. Gerald Westerbrook had a personal rule, which was never to take on another broker's problem accounts. He had developed this rule to address a common problem—the anger and resentment clients harbor for previous service providers spilling over to their dealings with the new providers. It's likely that Stinson had been bad-mouthing the old broker all over town, and would now likely do the same to Westerbrook. After all, he was a high-powered defense attorney who was used to verbally slugging it out with anyone who got in his way. And, frankly, people with huge egos often use others as punching bags.

The truth of the matter is that it can be nearly impossible to please a client who is still angry with another provider. And that anger can make that client toxic for years, and future service providers, to come. The frustrating and never-to-be-publicized fact was that Westerbrook really had done an excellent job with Stinson's account. But it was clear that Stinson simply didn't understand his account, and likely never really would.

Each industry and business has its own unique set of issues and strategies. In time, you will develop your own set of rules that apply to the practitioners and clients within your circles. But one of the rules that will apply to all industries and businesses is that the already-angry clients may stay angry with you, and through no fault of your own. Be careful when accepting such a client.

Chapter Three:

Lying

"One of the most striking differences between a cat and a lie is that a cat has only nine lives."
~ Mark Twain

Lies are everywhere. Governments are big and tell big lies. News outlets are far-reaching and can tell wide lies. Individuals usually stay in the smaller realm of lies but even they can tell some whoppers.

And lies never die.

With all this dishonesty you must gravitate toward the truth. You must work toward clients who are ethical, who won't waste your time and who will actually pay you for your time. You simply can't afford to have clients who lie to you and engage in deceitful practices.

The problem is, how can you ever know right off the bat whether they will lie and cheat? You can't.

A popular study reported in *American Psychologist* indicates that even those tasked with spotting liars—police officers, psychologists, and judges—were no better at identifying lies than the rest of us. In fact, only Secret Service agents fared better than random chance.

Meanwhile, a study published in the *Journal of Basic and Applied Psychology*, discovered that in a 10-minute conversation between two strangers, 60 percent of people lied at least once, with the average being three lies per 10-minute conversation.

Bottom line: You can count on being lied to. Knowing whom and what situations to avoid is not only crucial for your business but, ironically, it is gained only by being in business. A big part of knowing is relying on your instincts, which we will discuss further in Chapter Five.

But instincts can take time to develop. How can you know right now?

Part of the answer can come from the scenario you are in. As I've said before, getting a client is nice, but it's no excuse to let your guard down. You need to evaluate what the client says and what situation you're walking into.

Case No. 6: The Landscaper

Marvin Washington had a funny feeling about the family that hired him to build a patio garden at their country home. He couldn't put his finger on it, but for some reason Marvin didn't warm right away to the Collingsworths. They seemed respectable enough, though. Elena Collingsworth was a real estate agent. Her husband, Dexter, was a partner with his brother in a home supply-distribution company. They had two children and a dog. They had enough disposable income for an RV, dirt bikes and toy haulers, and, now, apparently enough to spend on prettying up the grounds.

Washington had recently begun his business as a landscape contractor. He held a college degree in horticulture and had bolstered his education with additional training in landscape design. He also was taking professional development classes in various aspects of landscaping, such as irrigation. Marvin was a full-service landscaper—designing and building projects, renovating gardens and performing limited landscape maintenance.

The only thing Washington lacked was years of experience. He was new to the business and only had a handful of clients. But the Collingsworths didn't seem to mind. In fact, they said they appreciated hiring someone new. Washington's sixth sense gave him some apprehension at that comment, but he needed the business.

"Back then, a small amount of money meant a lot," Washington said. "The landscape job was an $8,600 job, which could pay a lot of bills."

Today, after nearly two decades as a contractor, Washington has a strong, thriving business. He benefits from the fact that his reputation and customer base consistently generate good clients for him. Word of mouth is the best kind of advertising. Marvin's clientele for landscaping is largely self-selective. Washington's typical landscape client tends to be professional, well-educated, and upper middle-class—not rich, but with enough disposable income to afford his services.

It's not surprising, then, that what Washington calls his "crown jewel of miserable experiences" in business occurred toward the beginning of his career, before he'd carved out his niche.

The Collingsworths' home was nice but not pretentious, and sat in an idyllic pocket of the greater urban community: a "farmlet" area of winding lanes, green pastures with grazing livestock, pretty trees, ponds, and creeks.

The Collingsworths, by all appearances, could afford to pay for landscaping. They wanted a patio garden installed. Washington prepared a detailed written estimate for an area with interlocking pavement stones, several trees and shrubs, a drip-irrigation system, and bark mulch, all for $8,600.

Elena and Dexter Collingsworth accepted the estimate.

Washington and his assistant got to work. And almost immediately the Collingsworths became less and less communicative. In fact, while the work was being done, they had become rather distant and unfriendly.

Nonetheless, the job was finished on time and on budget.

Everything had seemed to go well until Washington and his assistant finished the work and it was time to pay.

Washington mailed off the bill, but several weeks went by and no check arrived. Instead, he was in for a surprise: On Christmas Eve, he received a registered letter stating that the Collingsworths had found the landscaping work "sub-standard" and had no intention of paying for it!

The letter, signed by both Elena and Dexter Collingsworth, stated that they didn't like the way the pavers had been installed, in addition to several other complaints. Washington was flabbergasted. A legal nightmare was starting, and he had no idea what would come of it.

Washington realized he was out of his depth. He knew that the small claims limit was only $5,000, precluding him from collecting the full amount. Washington did not know about mechanics' leins (discussed further on) and had not filed one.

Washington contacted his attorney, who helped him to sue the Collingsworths. The family then countersued, alleging that Washington had been working in their yard without their approval. In other words, they alleged he'd opted to work for free. Not only that, but while incomprehensively working for free, he had improperly staked the tree saplings.

The ugly legal dispute put the two parties before the judge three times, all in an effort to collect the $8,600 owed to Washington, plus $9,500 in legal fees (which would be over $20,000 in today's dollars). His lawyer told him "I've never experienced such a level of viciousness before."

But when all was said and done, Washington won, and both he and his lawyer were ultimately paid.

This leads us to the next important point about Toxic Clients: Some of them will purposely deceive you.

Since he was just starting in business and needed customers, it's likely that Washington appeared vulnerable—a quality that the Collingsworths were practiced at sniffing out.

While it can take some time to develop the instinct for spotting liars, every new business owner needs to consider whether that's precisely the reason they're being hired: Because they're new.

There is a class of Toxic Client out there who will take advantage of your limited experience in the business world. Your honesty and flexibility is seen by such calculating types as a vulnerability. While they will say that they like to give new business owners a chance, what they really mean is that they'll take a chance that new business owners won't know how to deal with their deceit.

This type of behavior is accentuated by the expense to resolve matters within our legal system. Most deceitful Toxic Clients know that it can quite easily cost $50,000 in legal fees to resolve a $10,000 dispute.

They know that the expense, combined with the stress and time commitment of litigation, makes it more likely for a new business owner (and sometimes even seasoned ones) to walk away.

How do you deal with this type of client? There are a few things you can do.

First, check to see if a potential client has been involved in litigation. You can go down to the county courthouse (or, in some cases, go online) to see if he or she has been involved in court cases previously. Typically, if the person has been a plaintiff (the person bringing the suit), they claimed to be unsatisfied with the work. While some grievances are certainly legitimate, it can also mean that the person bringing the case was using the court system to gain concessions.

If the person was a defendant, it's possible that they were sued because they never paid for the services rendered or products purchased.

A review of the county clerk's files to see whether your potential client is litigious, either as a plaintiff or defendant, can be very enlightening. If you are a contractor, a review of mechanics' lien filings (which can indicate a lack of payment for work performed) may also reveal a potential client's true colors.

Second, check the potential client's credit. You're probably used to having your credit checked when you apply for credit. But unless you are a landlord, you have probably never checked someone else's credit. That's because there are strict limits on who can check your personal credit reports. But those restrictions don't apply to business credit reports. Not only can you check the credit of someone you are planning on doing business with, it's a good idea for you to do so. There are several sources for checking business credit:

- Cortera
- Nav
- DNB
- Experian Small Business
- Equifax

You generally don't need your client's permission first, unless you are ordering a blend of reports that contain personal information about the owners or principals. The source you choose will depend on how much information you need and how much you want to spend. You can often get a single report for less than $100. It can cost you more than that if you wanted detailed information. But if you are going to spend time or money working with a client, don't you want to increase the odds you'll get paid on time and in full?

If you, as a new business owner, see a pattern (or even one instance) of nonpayment and/or litigation, you should probably think twice about taking the client. Or, perhaps, ask the client to explain the situation. ("I see you were sued by Marvin Washington. What happened?") How he or she answers the question hopefully will give you plenty of insight into the situation. You'll have to go with your instincts on the response: A calm, reasoned explanation may sway you one way, again remembering that none of us are all that good at identifying the liars in our midst, while an angry or defensive tirade might sway you in the other direction.

Another strategy is to develop a retainer program, if you don't already have one. You can ask for a 25% to 50% deposit on the work to be performed. The client who objects to this may be the client who had no intention of paying you in the first place, in which case you haven't lost anything by making the request.

Another strategy is to develop what is called the "imaginary partner." Many people starting out want to be pleasant and accommodating in the hope of gaining much needed business. In doing so, they will agree too readily to terms and conditions that are not in their best interests.

To slow this process down, and to give the semblance of experience in the business, create an imaginary partner whose approval you need. Instead of agreeing to everything on the spot, tell the client you need to take it back to your "partner" for his or her acceptance of the terms. You can add that your partner has a great deal of experience in these matters and will have a good sense of how to proceed.

This offers several advantages. First, it allows you to save face by not directly saying no to the client. Of course, more experienced business owners have no problem saying no, and you will get to that point. But until you do, it may be easier to make your "partner" the bad guy, which can allow you to come back and attempt to negotiate a more reasonable set of terms.

Another advantage of the imaginary partner is that it takes away the argument many Toxic Clients will use on new business owners: "You're the president. You can decide."

While the truth is that you are the president and can decide, sometimes decisions need a little time. I prefer to sleep on a big decision. Sometimes I need two nights' sleep. I am much better able to decide after a little time has passed.

The imaginary partner (or a real one, for that matter) gives you that time. It allows you to go back and consider things, rather than agreeing to them when you are vulnerable and exposed to what perhaps may be a more skilled negotiator.

To this end, I have worked with a number of clients who are starting their businesses and need to come up with titles for their business cards. We review whether they want to list themselves as "president" or instead list themselves as "vice president" or "manager." If you are going to use the imaginary partner strategy, having a card listing you as a lower officer fits right in. The card itself announces that there is a higher authority. It can certainly be to your advantage if the clients don't know that the higher authority is you.

I have other clients who feel they get more respect by listing themselves as president. And that is fine, as everyone's strategy is different. I would only caution that if you are young and starting out in business, the kind of Toxic Clients we are discussing here will want to see you listed as president. At least do yourself the favor of thinking twice about things when you hear the words, "You're the president, you can decide." In that vein, some of my clients who are the president have two sets of business cards printed up. One lists them as the president and one lists no title at all. They use each card according to the situation.

Of course, we have to reconcile one issue in this section on lying and deceit: In the imaginary partner strategy, you are lying. There is no other partner. It's just you.

Maybe you will have no trouble with it. It's your business, your baby, and you are trying to protect it from all the other liars and cheats out there. The justification is readily apparent to you.

Alternatively, you can simply say that it's "company policy," which technically is not lying since you establish company policies. But it does establish a higher authority that is immutable.

But maybe you need more of a foundation to support this strategy. Well, consider the German approach toward business. In Germany, a necessary lie is considered harmless. Here, the lie—that you have another partner and need that person's approval—is necessary to protect and grow your business. And if the lie is necessary, which it often is, then it is harmless.

Here's a final word on Marvin Washington's case. Early on, Washington had had a funny feeling about the Collingsworths. A little voice said to be careful. That was his instinct. He ignored his gut because he needed the work. The irony, of course, is that by ignoring his instinct he jeopardized his work.

So learn to develop your "lie sensor," and don't ignore it when it starts setting off alarm bells.

Lesson #3: Everyone lies. Don't let a lack of experience make you a target.

Often, people will actually tell you they are lying. Not in words, but in movements.

Think about all the nonverbal cues people throw off. You know them. They include:

- Fidgeting
- Avoiding eye contact
- Rapid blinking
- Rubbing the nose
- Swallowing repeatedly
- Clearing the throat
- Covering the mouth when speaking
- Wetting the lips

- Neck rubbing
- Scratching the head while talking
- Putting a hand to the throat

Many of these movements and mannerisms are crystal clear cues that a lie is being told. The speaker is not clear with their conscience and by fidgeting or the like they are subconsciously telling you so. Employ your lie sensor in such situations. Think twice – or more – about taking on what I call the 'kinetic client'.

That said, some people are genuinely nervous in certain settings. Introverts may be both honest and kinetic. As in all of our situations, nuance and discernment will benefit you.

Office Politics

Another type of deceit occurs in larger corporate settings, where a significant number of people spend an inordinate amount of time defending their turf. This can be problematic for the new professional walking into it, as our next case illustrates.

Case No. 7: The Graphic Designer

The gaming industry is extremely competitive as it is. But with Indian casinos and new mega-resorts cropping up all over the country in places new to gambling, fighting to lure visitors with glitzy expansions and high-powered promotions, the industry can be brutal.

The Thunderdome Hotel & Casino was preparing to open a new tower, and was eager to capture a bigger market share—especially with younger gamblers. Fresh ideas were needed to completely update the resort's image as a hip and sexy place to play. The Thunderdome's advertising and marketing department was staffed with longtime employees too stuck in their routines and habits to be truly innovative. They needed some new blood.

Courtney James, the department director, hired freelance graphic designer Marla Welch, a twenty-something woman who had graduated from a top art institute, was up to date on the latest graphics software, and boasted stellar ad pieces in her portfolio. Welch was given a three-month contract and a desk and computer terminal in the ad department, and was told to freshen up the advertising of the casino's new look.

Welch was excited that the contract with Thunderdome would give her a financial cushion. And she was eager to tackle the project. She was confident of her skills, and through her freelance career she had earned plenty of solid experience branding companies from the ground up—designing logos, creating business cards and other printed pieces, and developing all the aspects of marketing campaigns. Among her roster of former clients were a touring rock band and the NBA's Development League.

But if there was one thing she wasn't excited about, it was working out of the marketing office, instead of from home. That, she knew, meant she'd have to deal with attitude from territorial employees. She had experienced that before. With her short orange hair, green eyes, freckles, and an upper-register voice, Welch's youthful appearance often caused older people to disregard her experience or knowledge and get defensive about having their toes stepped on. This was certainly the case in the Thunderdome's marketing department.

One of Welch's first assignments was to supervise a photography shoot of high-end hotel rooms under construction. The photos would show off the luxurious features—plush feather beds, big HD TVs, heated towel racks, wet bars, large spas, and magnificent views. The photos would be used in brochures, magazine ads, bill- boards, and other signage. Since Welch wasn't yet familiar with the casino's layout, the ad depart- ment director assigned Pauly Tufts to assist Welch on the shoot.

Pauly was the man with the most seniority in the department. He was a pudgy man in his 50s who wore polyester clothes and a gold chain, and kept his gray hair feathered; his look instantly screamed "out of touch." Somehow he had man- aged to carve out a niche at work, handling all the television and radio buys and marquee designs.

Because of his many years at the Thunderdome, Pauly knew his way around the property. That's why Courtney, the ad department director, de- cided to give him a support role as facilitator for the photo shoot. He was to be in charge of the master set of keys and let the photography team and models into the rooms, muster up furniture and towels, and provide whatever other logisti- cal support Welch needed.

Harrison Browne, a freelance photographer, was hired for the day-long shoot. Over the phone, Browne, Welch, and Pauly agreed that the shoot would start at 9 a.m. the next day. "Don't worry about a thing," Pauly told Welch in a jovial voice after the conference call with Browne. "I'll get everything you need. Just show up at Room 1051 tomorrow morning."

When Welch showed up at the room in the new tower the next morning at 8:50 a.m., Browne greeted her cheerily. The two knew each oth- er from a previous freelance session and had worked well together. "We're just getting start-ed," Browne said.

Welch was surprised to see that the lighting had already been set up, but she didn't make much of it. The shoot got underway and looked to be ahead of schedule.

But Pauly kept trying to take over the shoot. He'd step in front of the camera as the photogra-pher was about to click the shutter, and say, "Oh, let's do this right here." He'd rearrange pillows on the bed. He'd adjust the window blinds, af-fecting the lighting. He'd tell the models how to pose, and his suggestions seemed awkward and inappropriate.

Welch and Browne grew increasingly flustered. At one point, Pauly took his comb from his back pocket and brushed a female model's hair.

"What are you doing?" Welch cried. "You don't touch the models!"

Browne finally had had enough. He pulled Welch aside. "You're the art director. You have the vision here. What's this guy doing?"

"I don't know what to do," Welch said. "I'm so frustrated right now."

"He's bugging the beans out of me," Browne said. "You've got to help us both out here. You've got to stand up and say something, otherwise this shoot is going to run a lot longer to get what we need, and I'm going to have to charge you more."

Welch immediately took an assertive approach. Whenever Pauly made a change, she immediate-ly stepped in and changed it back. "Actually, the lighting is this, and we need to have them here," she'd say. "Do you have a problem with this?"

A flash of anger would cross Pauly's face, but then his expression would shift to innocence. "Oh, no, sweetheart. Everything's fine. I'm just here if you need me."

The next morning, Courtney James called Welch into her office and shut the door. The director was furious.

"I can't believe you showed up an hour late for a photo shoot you were in charge of!" Courtney said.

Welch's face flushed. Her jaw dropped. "There was an obvious miscommunication," she stammered.

It turned out there had been a non-communication. Pauly had secretly arranged for Browne to show up at 8 a.m. to start setting up for the shoot. Of course, Pauly had not bothered telling Welch. But he'd made it a point to inform the boss that Welch had been tardy.

Welch realized she'd been duped.

"Before you yell at me, don't you think you should hear my side of the story?" she asked the director. "If you want to call Harrison, he'll tell you we agreed the shoot was to start at 9. He's a friend of mine. We've worked together before. He can vouch for me."

But James would have none of it. "From this point on, you're on probation," she said.

Welch's head spun. She considered resigning. But she decided to stick it out for the remainder of her contract. She couldn't afford to get a reputation as having failed on a job.

But Pauly kept up his sneaky attacks. He told James that Welch was regularly late to work. Then, after Welch had designed several logos, Pauly reported to Welch that one of them had been approved for use in advertising going forward. But it wasn't until, in a staff meeting, when James looked curiously at the ad mock-ups Welch had prepared and asked, "What's this logo? This isn't approved," that Welch realized Pauly had fooled her again.

"Well," Welch responded, "Pauly said this was approved."

"No, I didn't," Pauly said. A smile briefly flitted on his face. He was clearly playing her.

The stress this created for Welch threatened to make her sick. She was having trouble sleeping and her stomach felt upset at the prospect of returning to work each day. In bed at night, she considered quitting before the contract was up, but feared having word spread around town that she was an unreliable graphic artist, and that no one else would hire her. She had to do something, so she made a decision to take charge of the situation.

Knees trembling and voice shaking, she walked into James' office and kindly explained that she didn't need the Thunderdome as a client, but that she was interested in what it could offer for her portfolio. If they liked the look she was going for, James would have to make sure the employees backed away from her and stopped interfering so she could do her work.

Otherwise, she would not hesitate to leave.

By this time, the director had been keeping a close eye on Welch, and realized that Pauly had been up to dirty tricks. She apologized profusely for having exploded at Welch over the photo shoot, and begged Welch not to quit.

From then on, James took Welch to lunch every so often to make sure everything was going OK, and to gain insight into the work habits of her subordinates.

Interestingly, although it took some time, the resort's general manager had taken note of Welch's work on the redesign and was blown away. The simplified logo, new colors, updated brochure, the photo shoot ... the entire re-branding effort was remarkable. The Thunderdome now had a bold new look.

And when Welch's three-month contract was up, she was offered a permanent position in charge of continuing the redesign and other updates. Welch accepted the offer, optimistic about the improvements she had seen in the environment in recent weeks, but the arrangement only lasted a month and a half. The work environment continued to be stifling, and the undercurrent of office politics remained dispiriting.

When Welch resigned, the department director understood. "I knew this was going to happen," James told her. "You are so beyond here."

Welch had no regrets about leaving the Thunderdome and resuming her freelance career. And she is proud of how she handled the conflict with Pauly.

"What I have learned is that sometimes it takes being honest and harsh at the same time. It's not about being mean—it's about staying strong and true to your business. And that's how you last as a business."

As mentioned earlier, it's important to know the lay of the land when dealing with clients. What kind of situation are you walking into? Have you paid attention to the signals and listened carefully? Welch knew that the department's employees had been there a long time, and that their efforts were stale. That was a sign that people would be resistant to the change she brought with her.

Are you headed into a situation where the client will try to take advantage of you because you are new? Are you headed into a politically charged environment where employees are trying to protect their jobs, and will tear you down to build themselves up? Liars and cheaters are everywhere. By knowing the political and ethical landscape you are in, you will be more able to anticipate them.

Your lawyer, accountant and other professional contacts may also know about the reputation of certain clients. While attorneys have ethical rules as to talking about their own clients, many know the reputation of their non-clients. And most other professionals are aware of the bad actors in town.

Case No. 8: The Excavator

Burt Ditka was new in the excavation business. He had worked for a contractor for many years, until the contractor brought in his son to take over the business. Up until that point there had been an informal understanding that Burt would buy the owner out some day. That ended when the son got old enough to realize that his best move was to take over the old man's company. Burt realized *his* best move was to go into business for himself.

The owner had always said he would teach Burt the ins and outs of construction, but that never happened. They were always so busy working that the workings of the business were never explained. As a result, Burt didn't really know about Toxic Clients and the ways to get them to pay.

In his new business, on his third job, Burt learned very quickly. Jacob Hansel was a hard-nosed, well-heeled business man. He owned three nurseries and was expanding to a fourth location. Jacob contracted Burt for the excavation work on a challenging hillside at the new location.

Jacob had paid the invoices along the way without question. But when the final bill was submitted Jacob started complaining about the final improvements.

Burt went out to visit Jacob to try and settle the bill. When the businessman would complain about something Burt would explain how it was done properly. Reluctantly, Jacob said he would send in a check.

After 45 days Burt had still not been paid. He called Jacob on the phone to again ask for the final payment, Jacob said he'd been busy and would get to it. Burt said he was starting a big excavation job and wanted to get this matter resolved. With a harsh laugh, Jacob said he was glad to hear that Burt was busy.

Weeks later Burt was at a Little League baseball game watching his son play. Burt had come to know another father whose son was on the same team. The father was a lawyer. With two games a week at seven innings each there was plenty of time to talk.

Burt casually mentioned he had a local client who kept saying he would pay and then never sent a check. Knowing Burt was a contractor the lawyer asked when was the last time Burt had done work on the job. Burt thought about it and calculated it had been 89 days. The lawyer laughed and said Burt had one day left.

Burt was confused. "One day left?"

The lawyer explained that the best way for a contractor to get paid was to file a mechanics' lien. Such a lien placed a secured, priority interest against the client's property. If the client ever sold the property, the lien holder was paid first. In some states you had to bring a foreclosure action within one year of filing the lien in order to get paid.

But the key, the lawyer explained, was filing the lien within 90 days after the last work was performed. This, in Burt's case, meant it had to be filed the next day or he would lose a key point of leverage for getting paid.

The lawyer further explained that most savvy contractors and suppliers of products file a lien, sometimes called a Notice of Furnishings, at the start of a job. When it is not filed, a savvy land owner may sense that the contractor was not up to speed on all of the rules. By stringing a contractor out on payments for 90 days after the last work was performed, and past the lien filing deadline, the land owner could gain the upper hand. With no lien remedy available, the contractor may be forced to discount their bill in order to get paid, if they get paid at all.

The lawyer then asked the name of Burt's client. When told it was Jacob, the lawyer gave a bitter laugh and said, "That guy is toxic. He'd give an aspirin a headache. You need to come in tomorrow and we'll get that lien filed."

Beware of clients who will string you out with promises to pay so that you run past the lien filing deadline. A freeloader, or a feegoader (discussed ahead), who wants a significant discount for legitimate work performed will lull you to inaction through deliberate misrepresentations in order to gain later leverage. Don't give them such power. File your notices right at the start of the job. And then as soon as you finish the work file your Claim of Lien, which includes the first and last day of work, a legal description of the property and the amount owed.

We have included a brief overview of the mechanics' lien process in Appendix A. Please know that it is very general in nature and that rules vary state to state. There are a number of ins and outs, pitfalls and loopholes associated with these liens. Your best bet is to work with an experienced attorney in your area who knows the local rules. However, properly used, a mechanics' lien can get you paid.

One more point must be made about the old taking advantage of the young scenario. When I was a student at the University of California, Berkeley, I put together a student calendar. Each month featured a photo, a calendar with the academic deadlines and Cal sports schedule, and four ads along the bottom. I sold it on the premise that a company's ad would be in front of all these students for one month, and it only cost $90. I truly believed it was effective advertising. I spent all summer chasing down ads around the campus community. This was great for several reasons: I didn't have to work for anyone else, I got to work on my sales skills (which are important to have, no matter what business or profession you enter), and it allowed me to spend my summer break in Berkeley, which is as pleasant as can be in July and August.

One summer, I spoke with a crusty restaurant owner on the south side of the campus about advertising. He was about

70 years old, and I was 20. As I look back, I recall him looking at me as if I were another meat shipment to be cut up and served. He signed the advertising contract and asked to see a proof of the ad before we went to print, which I did for everyone anyway.

When the proof was ready, I went by the restaurant to get his approval. He was too busy to see me. I went back five more times, and he either wasn't there or wouldn't see me. Eventually, there was no time left; we had to go to print. I showed the proof to his manager, who gave his OK, and the ad was included.

The next week, I returned with a copy of the final printed calendar and an invoice. This time he would see me. He was angry that I hadn't shown him the ad. He told me that he didn't like the ad that we had printed and he had no intention of paying for it.

I was incredulous. "You're not going to pay me? You signed a contract. Your ad is right here!" I argued. This only angered him more, and he threatened to call the police if I didn't leave. Stubbornly, I retorted: "I'll call the police on you."

The old man smiled, and I'll never forget what he said: "They don't get involved in minor disputes. No one ever gets involved in minor disputes."

I was angry and bitter. But since I was entering my senior year, taking a heavy course load and trying to get into law school, I didn't have the time to pursue it. Of course, I told all my friends what a cheat this guy was, hoping it might at least cost the old man $90 in lost sales.

But the old man was diabolically right in this case. I didn't get further involved to collect my $90.

In my first year of law school, I learned what a great case I would have against this cheat. When I had gotten approval for the proof from the restaurant manager, it was as if I had gotten it from him. The manager was the owner's agent; he could give such approval and had. I learned the legal theory of quantum meruit, a Latin phrase meaning "what one has earned." In contract law, under quantum meruit you can recover for the reasonable value of the services you provided. The court can look to equity and good conscience in requiring a payment to be made. The restaurant ad appeared in the calendar, so he had received $90 in value. Courts would order him to pay in that scenario.

But we still have the issue of pursuing a claim for $90. To put the amount into an inflation-adjusted context, room and board at Cal in 1974 was $100 per month so it was real money. But at that time, I simply didn't have the time. I was trying to study my way into law school and my plate was way too full. I didn't have a spare minute to go after the owner.

Plenty of other entrepreneurs like you face the same issues. You've got to make payroll. You've got to finish that next job. You don't have the time to go after that lying son of a !#?!

Surveys show that only 4 percent of those who had not been paid by clients consulted attorneys, and only 2 percent took those clients to small claims court. People are too busy to fight to get paid. Unfortunately, the liars know this.

Today, I would pursue my claim against the old restaurant owner. People who cheat need to be hauled into court—not only to pay on what's owed, but to send a message that such behavior isn't tolerated. And to show that the legal system can, and should, be brought to bear against unethical behavior. We have included a guide to small claims court in Appendix B. Please read it so that you can be prepared to pursue what is owed to you.

In Marvin Washington's landscaping case earlier in this chapter, the parties went to court and Washington eventually won. The benefit to him was three-fold: 1) He received the money he was due, 2) There is a chance that the Collingsworths won't do it again to the next new business owner they come across, and 3) Going through the whole process makes Washington (and now you) a better and savvier business person.

Learning how the system works, how easy (and fun) small claims court really is and how you can promptly collect is a valuable skill. While we don't want Toxic Clients in the first place, we want to make them pay if we happen to do their work.

And that leads me to the next kind of Toxic Client: The kind that wants you to work for free or at a big discount.

Chapter Four:

Freeloaders
and Feegoaders

"I have never understood why it is 'greed' to want to keep the money you've earned but not greed to want to take someone else's money."
~ *Thomas Sowell*

"As I grow older I pay less attention to what people say. I just watch what they do."
~ *Andrew Carnegie*

Do you remember always working for free? This was a period of your life called 'school'.

Like me, didn't it bother you when the teachers loaded you up with all sorts of reports and assignments? You would have to go home and do all this work, and you'd have to do it for free! But you put your head down and did it all, knowing that someday you'd get paid.

When you finally were compensated for working it was frustrating to learn there were still teachers out there expecting you to work for free. In business, these latter day teachers are called freeloaders. You must learn to spot and avoid these people.

As mentioned in the first chapter, 80% of my clients have dealt with non-paying customers. Half have been stiffed by clients and 40% regularly deal with slow payers.

There is also a related type of Toxic Client I call the fee-goader. They will use every angle to goad, or pressure you to reduce your fee. As in the last chapter, by stringing out payment past the Mechanics' Lein filing deadline, a feegoader is a calculating and mean spirited client. You must keep your guard up against such types.

Freeloading and feegoading clients are everywhere. They force business owners to waste time and energy chasing after money that's rightfully due to them. To make matters worse, as the following story illustrates, unlike most teachers, freeloaders and feegoaders aren't that easy to spot. In fact, sometimes the people who appear to have plenty of money are the worst of all.

Case No. 9: The House Painter

Scott McGee painted houses for a living. He was good at it, delivering his service on time and on budget, and it had earned him a good reputation around town. His goal was to retire by age 55. He knew from his father that painting houses into one's late 50s took a big toll on that person's body.

In order to retire on time, McGee knew he had to make his margin on every client. He couldn't waste his time on the Toxic Clients who nickel-and-dimed, unreasonably complained, and tried to avoid payment. Over the years, McGee had developed a fairly strict system with his clients. He would bid the job, get a one-third deposit to begin the job, collect the next third when he was at the halfway point, and collect the final payment upon completion.

Two summers prior, McGee had bid on a job painting a house for Marcus Johnson, a well-known dentist in town. Johnson owned a large spread in the suburbs and wanted the job done while he and his family were on vacation.

The job was quoted at $18,000 and accepted. McGee collected the one-third deposit of $6,000 and began painting. When he was halfway done, he called Johnson for the next one-third payment. The dentist explained that he was out of town and couldn't get the payment to him.

McGee inquired as to whether Johnson's office manager could perhaps deliver a payment. Johnson offered several excuses as to why this option wasn't feasible. McGee was suspicious of the man's answers, but reasoned to himself that a rich dentist could certainly afford to pay, so perhaps there was no need to worry.

Johnson, as if reading McGee's thoughts, essentially said the same thing. He assured McGee that when he returned from vacation, he would issue prompt payment for the painting work.

As McGee had promised, the house was fully painted when the dentist returned home. But when Johnson arrived home he called McGee from his driveway to argue that the house had been painted the wrong color.

McGee was furious. Johnson had approved the color in advance, and had signed off on that color in the contract. How could it be wrong?

"It's a shade off," Johnson insisted. "It's not what I expected."

By now livid, McGee argued that every paint job had a slight deviation to it, that paint looked different in a can than it did on a house. The dentist would only say that it was not the color he wanted.

It seemed every time McGee made an exception to his established business policies, he ended up regretting it. The dentist had used McGee's failure to collect to his advantage. He told McGee that the house would have to be repainted to his liking.

Repainting the house would mean doing another $18,000 job, and McGee hadn't been paid in full for the first one. It would mean taking a huge loss. He told Johnson that he would do it if he received the remainder of the $12,000 he was owed. In a magnanimous tone, Johnson offered to pay $3,000 of the remaining $12,000 owed.

McGee angrily asked why he should accept $9,000 less than what the dentist had originally agreed to pay.

The dentist blithely replied, "Because it's the wrong color."

McGee knew the dentist had him. Normally, in a case where a client had paid the second deposit, he would have seen the color and the workmanship. Here, the dentist could argue that he had never approved any of it. He had been out of town.

McGee consulted with his lawyer and learned that in order to recover the $12,000 owed through legal action, it would cost him at least $10,000 in legal fees, not to mention the hours he would lose not being able to paint houses, which would put him even further behind. Plus, the lawyer said, it wasn't a sure thing that he would win.

As it turned out, after two lawyer demand letters, McGee received a $4,000 settlement from

Johnson, and took an $8,000 loss on the project. Of course, as McGee saw quite clearly every time he drove by the dentist's home, the house had never been repainted. Johnson was a feegoader who played the angles to goad McGee into reducing his fee. McGee was reminded of the lesson he'd learned long ago, which had prompted him to establish his payment policies to begin with. He vowed to never again make exceptions.

The fact that people appear to be rich and able to pay doesn't mean a thing. Frequently, the issue with Toxic Clients isn't money—it's ethics. Freeloaders and feegoaders (which we'll collectively call freeloaders for the rest of the chapter) place gain above principle. Of course Johnson could have paid for the house painting. He was earning an annual salary of hundreds of thousands a year. But when Johnson saw the chance to take advantage of the situation, he did so. The problem was that he had a toxic personality and was ethically challenged. For richer or poorer, he was flawed.

Lesson #4: Anyone can be a freeloader— even people who have plenty of money. Working for one is never worth it.

Freeloaders come in all shapes, sizes, professions, lifestyles, and income brackets. Consider all of the following scenarios— many of them may seem familiar to you. They all are examples of freeloaders:

A potential client contacts you about doing some work for him. He asks for numerous materials from you—a written proposal, sam-

ples of your work, references, ridiculously long introductory meetings followed by long follow-up conference calls … but still he offers
no real work.

This client is either milking your free advice or using your
time to get better terms from another vendor. You must determine at what point you're through putting in any more time,
energy, and ideas into the job until you are assured a contract
and payment. If it's this hard to get the client to hire you in
the first place, imagine how tough it would be to collect on an
invoice. This client has "toxic" written all over him.

*You're asked to do sample or "spec" work, for which you won't
be paid, to ensure you're a good fit. But somehow, the work is never
up to par, no matter how many hours you spend redoing it.*

Chances are that this client was using you to get free work.

Portfolios are intended to provide potential clients with
an idea of what you're capable of doing. But spec work is free
work, no matter how you look at it. Your ideas, your talents,
and your time are all valuable, and you shouldn't offer them
up to anyone who isn't willing to pay for them.

And think of it this way: If the client is this demanding
about free work, just think how much time you'll waste trying
to please him with the paid stuff. Is it worth all that work to
get a client like this?

*You're hired to do a job that you're really excited about. You've
signed a contract stating that you'll do the work at an agreed-upon
price, and you're confident about your ability to complete it in the
time allotted. But shortly after you get started, the client calls you
and says, "I forgot to tell you, but we need this other thing done, too.
Can you take care of that as well?" Before you know it, you're doing
twice the work you'd originally planned, and only earning half of
what it's worth.*

Before you know it, the size and scope of the job has completely changed, but, like that proverbial frog in a pot of water, you don't realize the water's boiling until you're cooked.

Before accepting any job, you and the client should spell out all details of the work in writing, with the caveat that if the scope of the job changes, other charges may be added to the agreed-upon price. And beware of vague language; sometimes clients use vague language so as not to reveal the true nature of a job, thereby getting away with paying less.

Ask for clarification on anything that isn't completely clear to you. And if you can't get a straight answer, you have a potentially Toxic Client on your hands. My best advice is to walk away.

One of your clients is keeping you busy ... too busy. In fact, his constant changes and updates are eating up all your precious time. But it's not making you any extra money. Until it's done, he won't pay you, but it seems it's never done because the client keeps changing his mind.

To me, this sounds a lot like the client is afraid of commitment, and that includes his commitment to paying you. This is a good reason why you need to spell out all details of a job beforehand, including how many revisions you're willing to include in the price. Anything above and beyond that should be added to the final amount.

A potential client contacts you about a job and asks for an estimate. You work up what you know to be a fair rate for such a job, but the client thinks this is an opportunity to try haggling with you over the price, and insists that he knows other people who will do the same work for less.

This client won't be happy no matter what rate you offer. In his mind, any number you start with is just a starting point, an invitation to start negotiating. He'll often taunt you by insisting that your competitor offered a better price.

Don't buy into this game. The focus should be on the value you provide for that rate, rather than price alone. Discuss the reasons for your prices. Mention the value added benefits of your work. (Again, this is where your sales skills come into play.) Assure him that you've set a fair rate, but if he truly thinks he can get the work done elsewhere for less money, he should probably go ahead and do it. The nonchalant mention that he should probably go elsewhere—the anti-sales pitch—is a solid and effective strategy. Start using it and you will see immediate results.

Know that it is very tempting to take the bait and accept less, especially if your money is tight. But clients like this usually take more time and create more stress than the rest. After all, he's not going to let you cut back on your quality, so you're only inviting a world of trouble into your door by taking him on. Whatever money you get won't really be worth it. And think of it this way: It also probably won't put you ahead of your competitors if you snag this guy's business. After all, do you really want to be known as the cheapest deal in town?

A client who, by all appearances, seems completely normal and pleasant, completely changes after you send your invoice. All of a sudden, everything in her life is falling apart and keeping her from being able to pay you—there's been a family emergency, she's been in the hospital, she was forced to pay the IRS for some unaccounted-for taxes, business has been slow and money's tight ... but she'll "put the check in the mail as soon as I can." You never receive it.

At one time or another, most business owners will deal with this client. The sad fact is that you likely won't receive this person's payment without pursuing legal action. Do you have a contract that you can fall back on? You must let this client know that if she doesn't pay what is owed to you, you will have to collect it by other means. As I've said before, I wouldn't hesitate to drag her to court for money that is due to you.

Small claims court is remarkably simple. You file a claim, have the defendant served and go in and tell your story. Back up your claims with evidence, bring in a witness or two if appropriate and be calm and polite. Anyone can do it. After you do your first one it gets so easy it becomes fun. I mean this. You are on stage fighting for justice. Be assured, you will come to enjoy it. And by the way, you'll get paid. (Again, be sure to read the small claims guide in Appendix B).

In any situation, having a written contract will most certainly give you a leg up. As Samuel Goldwyn once said: "Oral contracts aren't worth the paper they're written on."

Without a contract or something in writing indicating that you were hired to perform work for an agreed-upon amount of money, the judge has to deal with all the finger pointing of 'he said-she said.' With only an oral contract you will learn a very expensive lesson. You need a written contract.

As well, you should do your due diligence (investigative work) before accepting any client:

- Thoroughly discuss ALL details of any project, and have the client sign a written estimate detailing the work. If you can, collect a deposit or ask for a retainer, which ensures that the client has some skin in the game from the start.
- Research the client with the Better Business Bureau to determine whether any complaints have been filed against the client.

- Look into court files and business credit reporting agencies to discover whether the client has been involved in legal action or has bad credit.
- Don't be afraid to walk away if something doesn't feel right.

Some freeloaders have no intention of paying at the start. Others sense a weakness in your systems (such as lackadaisical or disorganized billing) and are encouraged to become freeloaders. Both are Toxic Clients. And both must know that you will use a collection agency to get paid.

There are over 4,000 collection agencies in the United States.

Clearly a lot of business owners need assistance in getting paid. A collection agency will keep 10% to 50% of what is collected. You most likely can't stay in business if every account you have is sent to collection. Still, you need to try and collect something on your hopefully few bad accounts, which is where collection agencies come into play.

Consider the following scenarios:

- A new customer does not respond to your first bill. You have no prior history of dealing with them. The odds are good right up front this will be difficult to collect.
- You agree to a payment plan but they don't follow through. Again, you are unlikely to collect.
- You later learn that a non-payer has a history of financial irresponsibility.
- One spouse blames the other spouse for the debt. You have no way of knowing whether the claim is accurate or legitimate.
- A customer disclaims any obligation to pay.

- A customer makes excuses not to pay due to poor service or a bad product.

The more time passes with such clients the less likely you are to collect. It may be prudent early on in this game to turn the debt over to a collection agency. Your time is most likely better spent creating new business than chasing after old accounts. Yes, by giving up, for example, 25% of what is collected to the agency you won't collect the full amount. However, by not using an agency there is a very good chance you will collect absolutely nothing.

We have included more information on how to use a collection agency in Appendix C. Know that millions of businesses use them to collect from millions of Toxic Clients.

Sometimes a matter is too small for collection, but just as toxic. Lyn Millard is the operations chief for my firm, Corporate Direct, Inc. She is the one who deals with clients and billing issues. While we greatly value and appreciate our clients, there are always a few…

Recently a client paid their annual corporate filings of $275 with a check from a closed bank account. The bank returned the check and charged us a $25 fee. When we finally traced down the client (more extra work) he would only pay the $275. Lyn asked why he wouldn't reimburse us for a $25 fee his actions forced us to pay. The client said that was a cost of doing business and that we should 'act responsible' and forego the fee. Lyn always keeps her calm, and she did here. But inside she was boiling. Act responsible?!? This from someone who wrote checks on a closed bank account!

But how much extra work do you want to put in over $25 dispute? To fire them as a client would involve refunding his

$275 and filing notice with the state. The administrative time was well over $25. The client probably instinctively knew this. What he didn't know is that we have a very good database. We put notes in his file about this problem. He will never get a second chance for an irresponsible act with us.

You may have heard of the 80/20 rule. Blair Singer mentioned it in the Foreword. It is formally known as the Pareto Principle.

Essentially, it states that 80 percent of your money is earned from 20 percent of your clients, while 20 percent of your clients account for 80 percent of the problems and time you spend dealing with them. You need to focus on the 20 percent of clients that are really paying your salary and are good clients, and find a way to jettison the folks that account for 80 percent of your problems. We will discuss how to dismiss Toxic Clients in Chapter Eleven.

The Customer is Always Right?

When it comes to blatant misuse of the overused adage above, freeloaders are among the worst. Like bears to a dumpster, when they get a taste of 'free' for complaining they will always return.

Case No. 10: The Tourist Shop Owner

A client of mine once made the mistake of giving away a free T-shirt. Jeanne Nakamura owned a tourist shop in a high traffic location. One morning a customer came in complaining that her XXL Lake Tahoe tourist T-shirt had shrunk to a small. The lady seemed earnest and nice enough. She said they were leaving in an hour, the shirt had been packed away and was wondering if Jeanne could please take care of it. Jeanne knew some T-shirts were defective. If the lady were telling the truth, Jeanne wouldn't want the T-shirt back. In this one case Jeanne didn't ask to see the T-shirt or look at the receipt, but instead took the mid 50's matron at her word.

We'd all like to do that—to be trusting and civil to all. But then again, no good deed goes unpunished.

The next afternoon three more ladies showed up, all complaining that their T-shirts had shrunk. Jeanne sensed a rat or, more appropriately, a rat pack. She asked to see their receipts for the purchase. The ladies all scoffed and said that no one kept a receipt for a T-shirt. Jeanne pointed to a sign on the cash register that said all returns must be accompanied by a receipt. The ladies grew angry at such unfriendly merchant logic.

The ringleader loudly stated: "The customer is always right! Our T-shirts all shrank and we all want new ones!"

The store was crowded with tourists and the brusque comment focused all attention on Jeanne at the cash register.

Jeanne kept calm, as she had been trained to do. She politely asked to see the shrunken T-shirts.

The ringleader said, "They shrank out of sight. We couldn't even bring them in."

Jeanne said she needed proof they had bought a T-shirt.

"The customer is always right!" repeated the ringleader. "You gave our friend a new T-shirt when hers shrank out of sight."

"I need proof of purchase," Jeanne said evenly.

"We're going to call the police," said another lady. "This is a fraud shop."

Several people were waiting in line to purchase merchandise. Jeanne decided to speak to them. "Is it alright if I charge all of you an extra $10 to accommodate these ladies? They have no proof of purchase and want free T-shirts."

A young man standing in line spoke up. "Are you ladies pulling a scam?"

"What!"

"Why should I pay more if you have no proof of purchase?"

With that the ringleader threw up her hands. "C'mon girls, let's go call the police on this lousy place." At the door she turned and pointed at Jeanne. "We're going to write some really bad online reviews about you!"

For ten seconds the store was silent. Everybody caught their breath.

The young man then said: "I never believe online reviews."

With that everyone laughed and went about their normal business.

The question raised in the story is one for you to ponder. Why should your regular clients have to pay more if you keep giving free stuff to Toxic Clients?

There is a cost to free, and that cost is borne by your good customers. They don't want to pay more for your products and services so you can hush the fake angry freeloaders. They shouldn't have to pay one extra cent for freeloaders. Don't forget your good clients when you are dealing with the bad ones.

As the story also illustrates, as you become known for giving away free stuff to complaining customers you will attract more customers complaining to get free stuff. Again, no good deed goes unpunished.

The classic freeloader example is the diner who complains of hair on his plate to get a free meal. In my youth I worked as a waiter at a country-style French restaurant in the fancy Georgetown district of Washington D.C. The area has since turned from nice commercial to over-the-top tourist. Back then, the owner of the restaurant represented American success. He had immigrated from France as a boy after World War II. He had no money, started as a bus boy, learned the business and worked his way up. He saved his money and opened his restaurant just as Georgetown was turning from a regular neighborhood into an elite one.

He could be gruff at times, but he had a good business to protect.

He had done well, in part by serving excellent food and also by never believing that the customer was always right.

I really enjoyed the work environment. As a general rule, the cooks were from French West Africa, the busboys were Asian and the kitchen staff was Latino. The waitresses were Georgetown foreign exchange students and pretty Persian girls whose families lost everything in the Shah's fall in Iran. It was like working at the United Nations.

The best seat in the house was a two top in its own cozy alcove looking out onto the bustle and great people watching of Wisconsin Avenue. For tips, that station was the prime one in the restaurant and I was glad to be working it one particular night.

A couple was sitting in the alcove and I took their order. I returned in 15 minutes with two crepes that the restaurant was famous for and set them in front of them. They each had a glass of white wine and were ready for a delicious meal.

Several minutes later the man called me over to complain. He pointed to a long black hair on his crepe. He said the cook must have been careless and he expected a free meal. In my early years, like some of you, I frequently spoke first and thought later. I blurted out: "The cook is bald!"

With this the man became very angry. He demanded to see the manager. Shaking my head, knowing I would somehow be in trouble, I went and got the French owner.

He had been to this rodeo before. He inspected the long black hair on the crepe. He politely said that the cook was bald and all the kitchen staff wore sanitary hats that prevented such a thing.

The man angrily pointed at me, "It must be from the waiter!"

Defensively, and again without thinking, I retorted: "My hair is short and blonde. The only person with long black hair is your lady friend sitting right there."

With this the man erupted, "What kind of restaurant do you run here? How dare you insult us like that!"

The French owner tried to mollify him. "Sir, let me get you another crepe. All will be fine."

The man was brusque. "This meal better be on the house!"

The French owner paused. He then spoke in a low voice. "If I replace the crepe, why should it be free?"

"Because your waiter insulted us."

"I am sorry," said the owner. "It doesn't work that way. When you order a meal here we expect you to pay for it."

With his bluff called the man got up and threw down his napkin. "Let's go Natalie!" He pointed to the owner. "I'm going to call the health department on you!"

The owner spoke politely "That would be Augie. I haven't seen him in a while."

The man was confused. "Augie…What's that?"

"Augie is our health inspector. Please have them send him in. I'd like to see him again."

With that the couple walked out in a huff.

I turned to the owner expecting to be fired. He smiled and counseled me to never get angry or defensive in such situations.

I nodded and again blurted out loud, "So I'm not fired?"

The owner again smiled. "Your instincts were right."

Relieved, I then asked if he worried that the couple would bad mouth the restaurant around town. I'll never forget his response.

"Nothing is worse than free."

When business owners, or entire industries such as food service, allow for free as a way to mollify real or imagined complaints all businesses suffer. More and more people become conditioned to complain and expect free. Instead, work on strategies to understand and deal with legitimate complaints. Then work on the strategies within your business, trade and/or industry to keep the freeloaders at bay.

Chapter Five:

Instincts

"Learning to trust your instincts, using your intuitive sense of what's best for you, is paramount for any lasting success. I've trusted the still, small voice of intuition my entire life. And the only time I've made mistakes is when I didn't listen."
~ Oprah Winfrey

"Common sense is genius dressed in its working clothes."
~ Ralph Waldo Emerson

As we have discussed throughout this book, experience as a business owner will enable you to determine more quickly which clients are toxic.

Until that sixth sense has a chance to become finely tuned, you'll probably first go through a period in which the potential of securing a new client causes you to see the world—and everyone in it—through rose-colored glasses.

But as Albert Einstein once famously said, "The only source of knowledge is experience." The initial discomfort you feel when you're about to do something dangerous, break a rule, or simply going against your nature or preferences often guides us in our personal lives.

However, for some reason, in business, we disregard it. We let money, notoriety, or the initial excitement we feel at being selected cloud our vision. We dismiss all the internal alarms that are flashing their warning lights at us, as we use the excuse, "But this is business."

Up until this point in this book, you've probably identified with many of these scenarios, but you probably also saw the trouble coming before our "heroes" did. You have probably seen it coming in your own personal life, too. But we're awfully quick to disregard our instincts when it comes to our livelihoods and businesses.

My point here is that all you really need to spot Toxic Clients is your own internal compass, the ability to recognize when it's sending you a warning, and a willingness to trust it.

Lesson #5: Your gut is your friend.

Trust it.

Tom Wheelwright is a nationally known CPA and the author of *Tax-Free Wealth*. He never forgets one big time he didn't trust his instincts.

"I was in a difficult spot in my business," Tom recounted. "We were growing quickly and I needed help."

Tom interviewed a top notch CPA who seemed to be a perfect fit for their expanding accounting practice. But the candidate insisted that he be a full partner in the firm right from the start. Tom's initial and immediate reaction, his first swift instinct, was to say 'no.' The CPA hadn't proven himself, and knew nothing of the firm's culture. Tom's instinct told him that the new hire was taking advantage of the situation. It was not a good start. But then the more prosaic concerns took over: "This is business. We need bodies. He'll probably fit in." The first blaze of instinct was overcome by the dulling day to day concerns of managing and growing a business.

"I should have followed my gut," Tom said. "Of course, in the long run this was never going to work out. The CPA did not fit into the culture. When he left four years later, it was not a pleasant parting. I have learned to trust my instincts since then."

Similarly, Mark Goodman, a Reno attorney, has learned to trust his gut after the first 'rich and famous' red flag client came his way. Now, with his instincts honed, he won't even take such a case. As Mark explained, "The client thinks that their case is my opportunity to make a name for myself and become rich and famous. The client is convinced that their case will be a sure bet to be covered in the national news and will therefore launch my career to new heights. There are a number of problems with these clients. The client may be delusional or at least unrealistic. There will surely be bitterness when their vision is unrealized, no matter how much I counsel against that expectation. As well, sometimes these clients are scheming to get me to take the case on more favorable terms (or even free) based on the assumption that having my name on this case will make my career. While it's true that there are some legal cases that become national sensations, these cases represent only a handful out of thousands and thousands. Let your instinct guide you away from such clients."

The Danger of Desperation

If you've had a Toxic Client before chances are that, when you're really honest with yourself, you'll realize that something about working with the client felt wrong from the start. The work seemed out of the ordinary, the budgetary requirements of the client seemed odd, the language the client used seemed vague and hard to understand, the client wasn't responsive to you on a regular basis, or something else altogether felt wrong to you. And it's likely that you went ahead and accepted the work anyway because you needed the money.

Case No. 11: The Marketing Firm

For nine years, Sandy Roth owned Aspen Mountain Marketing.

Her one-person firm provided advertising, marketing, and public-relations solutions to both small and large companies. The firm's clients included, among others, a disposal company, retail outlets, a soft-drink distributor, and a real estate agency.

In one of Roth's first marketing jobs out of college, she'd worked with Tom Golding, who was at the time a middle manager for a company using Roth's employer for its marketing. These days, however, Golding was CEO of Prompt and Caring, a chain of health care clinics. Golding's corporation was aggressively buying up independent practices. It now had more than 100 clinics throughout the West. Unfortunately, each office had its own brand. Prompt and Caring needed a single brand and consistent advertising. Golding asked Roth to submit a bid on the account.

Golding's corporation was prepared to spend up to $5 million per year on advertising in each of the first two years of the relationship. It would be a two-year contract with a chance to renew. Whichever agency landed the account would be paid a retainer, plus 15 percent of the media buys, and have its expenses covered.

The wheels spun in Roth's mind. This was the sort of account she could build a larger agency around.

She recruited three partners from her circle of advertising associates, and together the four prepared a pitch to make to Prompt and Caring. They agreed that if they landed the account, they'd form a new agency together, with the account as the anchor.

The four partners flew to California and gave an extensive PowerPoint presentation to Prompt and Caring's board of directors. The vote was 6-5, with Roth's team edging out the incumbent agency. Roth's instincts told her that the narrow margin of votes from the board meant her agency's work would be closely scrutinized by them—especially since one of the directors had been good friends with all of the owners of the incumbent agency.

Roth and her three partners were elated to have the account, but were almost immediately greeted with a surprise after the contract was signed. The board members said they'd overestimated their company's financial situation. They cut the ad budget to $3 million a year. Again, her instincts were alerted to potential future trouble.

The partners were somewhat disheartened, but reasoned that $3 million a year was still manageable. They were optimistic for the future. Without much reflection they took out a three-year lease on a large office space and hired three support staffers. Their monthly expenses went up, but the Prompt and Caring account would cover them.

The partners and staffers got to work creating a single brand for the health care chain, starting with the logo. They made the ad campaign consistent and hit each local market in which Prompt and Caring had clinics, buying television and radio time and billboard space, and placing print ads in newspapers and magazines.

Then a major snag surfaced. The hostile director who had voted against hiring Roth's agency because of his friendship with the former agency was promoted to chief operating officer—the number-three person in the company, behind only the CEO and CFO. This executive carried extra clout because he had been with Prompt and Caring longer than the CEO or CFO.

He proved uncooperative right away, dismissing any internal marketing strategy that Roth and her team suggested, and criticizing all facets of the ad campaign. Roth heard complaints from other people that he did not value ideas unless they were his. Roth said others called him "a control freak."

Eighteen months into the contract, on October 15th, Prompt and Caring exercised its 30-day out clause. To add insult to injury, it effectively ended the contract on Nov. 15—cutting out half of November's retainer.

Reeling from having their contract canceled with Prompt and Caring, the client they had built their agency around, Roth and her partners were now scrambling. They had a large lease obligation and a monthly payroll to make. They desperately needed to drum up new business.

Two weeks later out of the blue they received a phone call from a representative with St. Anselm's Healthcare, a company based in the Midwest. The company had recently purchased a midsized hospital in Montana, and was in the midst of a major makeover of the facility along with a re-branding into the St. Anselm's chain. The company was interested in meeting with Roth and her partners to discuss marketing opportunities. They set up a conference call for the next day.

During the call, the healthcare company's executives explained that they were unhappy with the advertising/public relations firm out of Montana that they'd been using, and said they wanted another agency to "manage" this first agency, though the implication was that the first agency would be fired if a new firm could get the job done. The executives needed to hire this new firm quickly.

But then things became even more complicated. The new agency would not only be working with the original agency (at least, at first), but also with the hospital chain's regular ad agency, which was based in Chicago. So from the start, three agencies would be working on the account.

It would be a 90-day contract, handling the re-habbed hospital's grand opening and accompanying publicity.

Roth was concerned about the complexity of the relationships. Her instincts again said problems could lie ahead. But the agency needed the business and needed it now. Roth knew they could certainly manage the rebranding of the hospital facility—handling media buys, public relations, and special events. And all the partners agreed they could use a new income source after losing the Prompt and Caring account. They assured the St. Anselm's executives that they were up for the challenge, the healthcare company's people agreed it was a good fit, and Roth's firm was hired that very day. A handsome retainer was offered.

The first Montana agency was, indeed, pushed off the project.

Then, two weeks into the job, the healthcare company's executives gave Roth the word that they were unhappy with their agency back in Chicago as well, since that firm "charged too much." Before long, the Chicago agency was fired and Roth and her team became responsible for the entire account, with the assurance that the 90-day contract could be renewed at the end. It had the potential to be a multimillion-dollar account.

The day they started, they were three months behind. Roth's instincts again said something was wrong. Still, as professionals the partners and their employees started working days, nights, and weekends to get up to speed.

Roth and her partners' enthusiasm meant they did not hesitate to return emails to the client's executives, no matter what time of day or night. The executives very quickly became accustomed to such quick attention and started expecting it, often emailing Roth at 6 o'clock in the evening to ask for a media plan or ad mock-up for the next morning. And though they held executive positions, they had poor people skills. The small things, like making demands without even saying "please" or "thank you", grated on Sandy's hard working group. They often belittled the job that Roth and her team were doing, and acted as if anyone could do marketing if they had the time.

Something else bothered her. Although St. Anselm's always paid Roth's agency on time, when

Roth placed ads in newspapers or other media, the St. Anselm's people who were managing the hospital project would pay for the ad with personal credit cards instead of checks. This told her that there were financing problems, and that their cash reserves were not what they said they were. She began insisting that St. Anselm's people pay 50 percent up front on printing jobs, and that the client pay (where the commissions were still honored) for the media directly, instead of billing it through her agency.

The contract's 90-day period drew to an end. The St. Anselm's executives told Roth that they loved her agency and wanted to continue working with her, at which point she drew up a new contract for them to sign. But after a few days, she received a voicemail message from St. Anselm's saying "We've decided to go in a different direction." Losing the two Toxic Clients so quickly was painful at first, but Roth soon realized that it was a double blessing in disguise. Her stress levels dropped and she was able to start spending more time with her kids, who noticed her mood improving.

On the financial front, Roth and her partners endeavored to put their agency on a more sound footing by cutting expenses in the partnership, so they could turn away problem clients and make sure their eyes were open when those clients showed up.

Roth is very clear about this experience, "A mentor once told me, 'Never make any decision based solely on money. It will almost always bite you when you do.' My instincts were correct on both clients. But I was blinded by the opportunity."

Your instincts are formed from a variety of things—past experiences, your knowledge or study in a particular area, your common sense, and your emotions. So finely honing all of these things, and paying attention to each one's merit, can help you to learn to listen to and trust that "still, small voice."

Your instincts can be brought forward for your benefit. Consider the following steps:

- Take note of prior experiences, and be cognizant of the lessons they have taught you.

- Immerse yourself in the study of your profession and your marketplace, so that your knowledge of your profession runs deep.

- Realize that you rely on your common sense to get you through the day; it will steer you right in business, too.

- Remember that your emotions are shaped by thoughts and experiences. If something makes you feel uncomfortable, there's likely a good reason for it.

Actively hone your instincts and then be sure to recognize them. A sure sign of a Toxic Client is the one you dread hearing from. So ask yourself:

Whose name do you cringe at when you see it in your inbox, or on your phone's caller ID display?

Which client will you do almost anything to avoid?

Which client, or potential client, gives you a bad feeling in the pit of your stomach?

Which potential client seems odd in a way you can't put your finger on?

Which client takes up 80 percent of your time and yet contributes to only 20 percent of your business?

Which client seems to have problems communicating effectively — leaving out essential information, speaking in vague terms, saying rude things, saying nothing at all, or speaking ill of others?

Which client makes you feel insecure or powerless?

It is often said that experience is the cruelest teacher. It gives you the exam first and the lesson later. But as you gain experience you will also come to refine your instincts. And in applying those instincts you will have fewer clients you dread hearing from.

There is an old German proverb which holds that: "Mistrust carries one much further than trust." Such mistrust is an instinctual reaction, a reaction that has helped mankind to evolve and succeed over eons of time.

From animal predators to warring tribes to now flawed individuals, our instincts have been honed to protect us, and continue to do so. Don't discount them. They are deep within you, at the core of your being. You will feel them in a jolt, and hear them in a little voice. They are true and insulating and must not be ignored.

Chapter Six:

Mental Health

"People think of the Golden Rule as something mild and innocuous,
like a baby lamb. But when they suffer an infringement of it, they
think they've been mauled by a panther."
~ Francis Wren

As we have discussed, a number of client situations present unique difficulties to business owners. Some clients don't abide by ethical norms and defy the standards of business conduct. But it also may be that some of our clients have their own internal troubles.

Mental Illness
Mental illness is fairly common in the United States and many other countries. It can range from insignificant to mild to a significantly disabling impairment. It can present itself as an emotional, behavioral or mental disorder. The National Institute of Mental Health recently estimated that 18.5 percent of all U.S. adults over the age of 18 had some form of mental illness. This estimate does not include the millions of people with drug, alcohol and other substance abuse disorders. (We will deal with those clients in the next chapter.)

With nearly 20% of the country affected by some disorder, it is imperative to recognize and be prepared to deal with the impaired client. Mental illness comes with no racial or economic markers. Even trained psychologists and school workers don't always see it coming. There are many high functioning individuals who appear untroubled. Until they are.

Personality disorders are an individual's emotions, behavior and thoughts which differ from societal norms. They most certainly differ from the way you want to conventionally operate your business. So it is important to know these disorders by name. Medical experts classify them into the following groups:

- Antisocial personality disorder: Manipulating, exploiting or violating other's rights.

- Avoidant personality disorder: Excessive shyness, inadequacy and fear of rejection.

- Borderline personality disorder: Unstable and turbulent emotions, actions and relationships.

- Dependent personality disorder: Excessive dependence on other people.

- Histrionic personality disorder: Acting emotional or dramatic to draw attention.

- Narcissistic personality disorder: Inflated ego and an obsession with self.

- Obsessive-compulsive personality disorder: A preoccupation with rules, orderliness and control.

- Paranoid personality disorder: Unfounded distrust and suspicion of others.

- Schizoid personality disorder: Feelings of social isolation and indifference to people.

- Schizotypal personality disorder: Difficulty with relationships and irregular lifestyle patterns.

Just as these groups are very diverse, the afflicted individuals can display a wide range of symptoms and severity. The next case illustrates the problems and the manipulations business owners face:

Case No. 12: The Beauty Salon

Jenna Starr thought she'd seen it all after nearly two decades in the industry. She knew the cosmetology field inside and out; she had grown up in the business, with a mother who was a hair stylist. Jenna earned cosmetology certificates in hair styling and skin and nail care. She had worked as a cosmetologist for 14 years before opening her 2,400-square-foot salon and spa, utilizing 20 independent contractors in addition to four support staffers. Business had been brisk since day one. The salon/spa, which provided hair, skin, and nail care, as well as massage, had built up a solid customer base with 80 percent repeat business. Appointments typically were booked four to eight weeks out.

But as experienced as she was, Jenna had never encountered a client as unique as the one the stylists called "No Filter Shirley."

Shirley was apparently wealthy. She drove a luxury car, and once even arrived at the salon wearing a full-length sable coat. Shirley could afford the expensive hair colorings and styles.

Shirley was in her mid-40s, had naturally curly blond hair, an average build, and plain features. While her appearance wasn't out of the ordinary, her behavior certainly was. For example, while getting her hair done, she would often make loud, off-the-wall comments, such as, "I wish dogs were more like cats so I could eat them."

Shirley became a regular client with irregular habits. Sometimes she'd show up for her appointment, sometimes she wouldn't. After being stood up three or four times, her stylist removed Shirley from the schedule book and wouldn't take appointments with her anymore.

The stylist believed that this took care of the situation, but because she hadn't brought the matter to Jenna's attention, no one else knew that Shirley was no longer welcome. And Shirley herself wasn't ready to give up on this salon. She called and made an appointment with a different stylist.

This time, Jenna happened to be cutting hair when Shirley came in. The new stylist led Shirley back to her chair. On the way, Shirley stopped in front of another stylist's chair, pointed at the woman having her hair done there, and exclaimed, "I don't like her hair. I don't want you to make me look like her."

This made the client and several other people in the salon who had heard the comment extremely uncomfortable. Jenna kept her eye on Shirley as her appointment proceeded. Jenna noticed that as Shirley sat having her own hair done, she complained loudly about her previous stylist.

After Shirley left, Jenna conferred with her stylists and learned about Shirley's pattern of abnormal behavior. Evidently, this woman had a habit of criticizing other customers' hair. Her prattle during appointments seemed to have no rhyme or reason. She spoke without filtering her thoughts. She was an intrusion for others around her.

But Shirley's new stylist had just started in Jenna's salon. She wanted to keep Shirley as a client, at least until she built up her own clientele. Jenna reluctantly consented.

On a subsequent visit, Jenna heard Shirley babble about her background, explaining that she was a nurse at the state mental hospital five miles away. Then she began railing about some of the patients there, and creating quite a disturbance. Jenna walked over and politely asked Shirley to tone it down, and the woman did eventually quiet down.

As coincidence would have it, another woman who was having her hair styled in the salon had a relative who was a patient at the same mental health clinic. She knew just who Shirley was. She called Jenna into a back room. "My brother is a patient at that clinic," the woman said discreetly. "That woman who was just here is also a patient. I've seen her there." She explained that Shirley had some sort of personality disorder that caused her to make socially unacceptable comments.

When Shirley's hair was done that day—a two-and-a-half-hour job complete with coloring and highlights—she told the stylist, "Oh, I'm sorry, I can't pay you today. I went out on the town and spent all of my hair money. I'll pay you at the end of the week." Then she turned and went on her merry way out of the salon. The stylist was distraught, believing she'd never see the $120 owed her.

But Shirley did come in a week later, and paid cash, which enabled her to continue on as a client at the salon.

On her next appointment, Shirley brought her Shih Tzu. Jenna wasn't in, but the receptionist explained that the owner prohibited dogs on the premises because of local health regulations. The health department could fine the business $5,000 if a dog was in the salon.

"Oh, she's a liar," Shirley said about Jenna. "She just hates animals."

While she had her hair cut, Shirley let her pet run around the salon floor.

The next time she showed up with her fluffy dog, Jenna was present. She told Shirley the dog had to stay outside. Shirley threw a fit, insisting that she could not possibly lock the dog up in her car. "I'm canceling my appointment," she snipped. She scheduled a new date for a haircut and left.

The stylists in Jenna's salon try accommodating clients' quirks, and make every attempt not to discriminate. But when Shirley didn't show up on time for her next appointment, her stylist had had enough. By the time Shirley showed up a half hour late, the stylist had left to run errands.

Jenna held a brief staff meeting about Shirley. All agreed that she was too much trouble to deal with.

When Shirley next called to make an appointment, the receptionist said her stylist was overbooked. Shirley didn't get the hint though, and continued to call.

Finally, Jenna phoned Shirley and explained that the stylist would no longer take her business, period. Jenna reviewed the issues: "We just can't please you. You often complain loudly about your hair. You speak in a negative way about people while you're here, and it makes people very uncomfortable. You've missed appointments and have frequently been late on payments. You've brought your dog in, against our salon policy, and then you claimed I lied about what the laws are. I'm sorry, but there have been so many problems with you that we simply can no longer keep you as a client."

Shirley responded contritely, trying to worm her way into Jenna's good graces. "I didn't mean to call you a liar," Shirley said apologetically. "I did check into it after that, and you're right. You can't have a dog in a salon."

Jenna stood firm. "Thank you, but we still won't be able to accommodate you."

Shirley was not ready to give up, though. A few days later, she called and used an alias, "Monica," to set up an appointment with a different stylist. The receptionist recognized Shirley's high-pitched, clipped Maryland-Merlin accent. The receptionist gave Jenna a signal that Shirley had called. Jenna called Shirley back. "I'm sorry," Jenna said. "As I explained before, you'll have to find another salon. We can no longer have you as a customer."

Shirley was surprisingly calm. "Thank you," she said. "I appreciate your honesty."

A month later, Shirley showed up at the salon. Jenna was ready for battle.

"Don't worry," Shirley said. "I'm just using my gift certificate. I'll just buy product."

Then, demurely, she added, "Will you please cut my hair?"

"No, I can't take new clients," Jenna said.

"I'm sorry," Shirley said. "I didn't mean to burn any bridges. I'll be nice. I won't be mean to anybody."

Jenna understood that Shirley had probably been banned from every other salon in town, and felt sorry for her. But she couldn't let history repeat itself at her establishment.

"I'm sorry, I just can't do it," Jenna said.

"I ticked you off, didn't I?" Shirley said.

"Yeah, you did," Jenna said. "You've upset too many people here. You can buy your products and use your gift certificate."

Shirley bought some items and left.

The staff knows that if she ever returns, the answer to scheduling her again always is no.

At least 10 percent of Americans will need treatment for some form of mental illness in their lives. Given the large numbers, some will become your clients. An organization known as Dementia Friendly America has launched a website at dfamerica.org to help businesses deal with clients exhibiting dementia and memory loss. These "dementia friendly" efforts may become a template for many communities.

Tolerance and patience in dealing with challenged customers is a good thing. But mental health issues are on a spectrum, and at some point you may not be able to assist. It is not your fault and it is not really their fault. They can't always respond to reason, and can't control their behavior. That is simply their chemistry. You must be aware of this. But even though it may be a faultless situation, it should not become your problem.

Psychologist, entrepreneur, and author Kenji Sax summed up this type of client in his book, *Get off the Couch! Seven Psychological Secrets of Success in Business* (SuccessDNA, 2003). In this book, he writes:

There are those few individuals who have mental illness, which often makes them generally angry no matter what the circumstance. In the elderly, some cases of severe dementia can bring about hostility and paranoia. Infrequently, other disorders such as schizophrenia and mania can result in similar behavior. For these individuals, there is very little you can do to make a difference in their perception of the customer service, nor can you always reduce their anger and frustration.

Sax, who has a Ph.D. in psychology and experience working in mental hospitals and other clinical settings, also writes about Borderline Personality Disorder ("BPD"). This is an important disorder for business owners to be ready to defend against. The fury can arise in an instant.

People with BPD can seem friendly and functional. But under the surface they may have trouble maintaining healthy relationships, a fear of abandonment and a poor self-image. No one is certain of the causes leading to this complicated disorder. But accepted theories include:

- A dysfunctional family environment: Families in which children are neglected, abused or abandoned can contribute to BPD.

- Hereditary factors: Some believe there is a genetic explanation for BPD.

- Brain issues: Abnormalities in key areas of the brain and/or a chemical imbalance of certain neurotransmitters may be a cause.

Whatever the cause, you must be prepared for a rapid change in mood. Calm and content can suddenly switch to inappropriate and uncontrollable anger.

The trigger for the BPD client's instant fury is a sense that they've been wronged. Disappointment or frustration will set them off. And it's as if they were waiting for an excuse to explode. Sax explains: "They have an expectation they're going to be let down. They have a persecution complex. They feel the world is not fair to them. If, all of a sudden, they feel like they've been wronged, their rage can rise in an instant."

Borderline clients have a tendency to see people as either wonderful or awful. When you, the service provider, go from being loved to despised the transition is quick. You may not know what hit you.

Lesson #6: There's no black and white when it comes to Toxic Clients. Every situation is unique, and those with mental health issues require extra finesse.

Dr. Sax emphasizes the importance of having systems in place to manage client expectations—and mitigate complaints from the few customers who express dissatisfaction. In some cases, it means refunding the clients' money and sending them on their way.

Sometimes this is the only rational way to handle a mentally ill client. In Jenna Starr's case, she handled Shirley the best way she could, in order to avoid taking on Shirley's problems too closely. While it may be tempting to engage such a person in a dialogue about the situation and whether that person's behavior was right or wrong, it may only exacerbate the problem to a point that might even be dangerous. Some people may become extremely agitated in any discussion of right vs. wrong.

Dr. Sax offers the following tips for providing customer service to someone showing the signs of a mental illness:

- Mental illness has nothing to do with intelligence. Don't assume people with such conditions aren't smart or will believe anything you say.

- Be respectful to the person. When someone feels respected and heard, he or she is more likely to return respect and consider what you have to say.

- If the person is experiencing events like hallucinations, remember that this is that person's reality, and you cannot talk the person out of believing his or her reality.

- Some people with paranoia may be frightened, so they may need more body space than you do. Observe personal boundaries.

- It's a good idea to set limits with such a person, such as saying, "I only have five minutes to talk to you" or "If you scream, I will not be able to talk to you."

- Call for help (police, security, or colleagues) if you feel physically threatened or need help de-escalating the situation.

If you can help such a person that is great. If you cannot you must be realistic. While it is honorable to be sensitive to the challenges of others, you are not in business to over accommodate those with their own personal problems. You cannot stay in business by allowing every customer's problems to become your problems. Additionally, the well-being of your staff must be considered. They are more important than any single customer. You should never put them at risk by allowing any matter to escalate out of hand.

If a situation appears too difficult to control, it's a good idea to extract yourself from it. In Chapters Eleven and Twelve, I'll share with you some tips for dismissing clients of all sorts, including those with mental illness, as well as tips for avoiding such situations altogether.

Chapter Seven:

Drugs
and Alchohol

"Drugs are a bet with your mind."
~Jim Morrison

"As an alcoholic, you will violate your standards quicker than you can lower them."
~Robin Williams

Have you ever heard the term 'Addictive Personality'? If Joe abuses drugs and alcohol some will simply conclude that he has an addictive personality.

But are there personality traits associated with addiction? While addictive personality is not a recognized psychological diagnosis, those in the field have certainly noticed common traits found in people with dependency issues. Those with addictions may:

- Appear very anxious and impatient
- Seem angry and intolerant
- Show signs of depression
- Have trouble waiting for delayed gratification

As you dig deeper, and as the studies show, many of those with addictions also suffer from some of the personality disorders we discussed in the last chapter. While not every addict has a personality disorder and not every person with a disorder is an addict, many suffer from both afflictions.

The two most common disorders associated with addiction are the Antisocial Personality Disorder (which traits include reckless behavior and a lack of responsibility) and Borderline Personality Disorder (which includes a fear of abandonment and a tendency to see people as either wonderful or awful.)

That said, there is no common portrait of an addict, or an addict with a personality disorder. They are not all drinking from brown paper bags and shooting up with used needles down by the train tracks. Indeed, many of them live in nice houses and are your clients.

You need to be prepared to deal with them.

Drug Abuse

We should all be angry at the Mafia.

As fictionalized in the movie "The Godfather", there was a moral debate within the Mafia about whether it was right to flood the country with drugs. Alcohol and prostitution were one thing, mere innocent vices in their view. But spreading addiction and despair across the land - well, even the Mafia had to wrestle with the ethics of that one. In the end, it was right for them from the standpoint of generating huge amounts of illicit revenue. As is not uncommon, money trumped morality. But the Mafia's decision wasn't right by the millions of lives that have been destroyed by drug usage. It wasn't right for the country.

'Made guys' now will tell you it would have happened anyway. If the Mafia didn't do it the Latin, Asian or some other cartel would have done it later anyway. The genie was doomed to come out of the bottle at some point. So deal with it.

And deal with it we will as, unfortunately, we must.

The connection between drug abuse and personality disorders, as mentioned, can be interconnected. In certain cases, someone with a personality disorder will self-medicate to reduce or stabilize their condition. In turn, they will become addicted. In other cases, extreme drug usage can bring forth a personality disorder by altering brain chemistry. In each case they are now both addicted and suffer from a disorder.

It is not your job as a business owner to psychoanalyze such people. In fact, some professionals caution that doing so can create more problems. But you need to know how to deal with addictive personalities, in whatever form they present themselves.

After briefly discussing alcohol abuse we shall explore strategies for dealing with drug and alcohol users.

Alcohol Abuse

Alcohol is the most used and abused substance in America. It is estimated that one in every 13 adults either abuses alcohol or are full alcoholics. The cost to society is enormous. From injuries, traffic accidents and health care costs to lost productivity and family disruptions, alcoholism is an economic drag of many billions of dollars per year.

The National Council on Alcohol and Drug Dependence defines alcoholism as follows:

> "Alcoholism is a primary, chronic disease with genetic, psychological, and environmental factors influencing its development and manifestations. The disease is often progressive and fatal. It is characterized by impaired control over drinking, preoccupation with the drug alcohol, use of alcohol despite adverse consequences, and distortion in thinking, most notably denial."

Denial is understandable. Most people have a drink and feel relaxed, even happy. The brain remembers these feelings and wants them continued. Given the right mix of factors, including family history, an individual may want these pleasant feelings to continue unabated. As the addiction takes hold, the person denies any change in their behavior. In their newly pickled mind, drinking is the same as eating – a necessary day-to-day function. They rationalize (and underestimate) their intake and are soon blind to their lack of judgment, uncontrollable anger and inability to think clearly.

Like the drug user, as an alcoholic, the individual is now addicted.

Addiction is, at its core, an uncontrollable drive or compulsive need to seek out and use drugs or alcohol at the expense of relationships, work, and activities of daily living. Given that it is a disorder that is often chronic or recurring, for most people long-term abstinence is required to reclaim and maintain a healthy lifestyle.

Psychologists and psychiatrists view drug and alcohol addiction from several perspectives. For example, there are people who use drugs because they are curious, or novelty sensation seeking. These people tend to "stumble" into addiction. Then there are the ones who use because of some underlying cause that drives them toward self-medication with illicit or prescription drugs or alcohol. Either way, the resulting addiction presents the same challenges and effects on quality of life. Researchers and clinicians try to understand and help people with addiction using two approaches:

Biological – This perspective looks mainly at the physiological drive to addiction and the subsequent biological systems like neurotransmitter and hormonal changes that take place in the brain and other areas of the body.

Psychological – This view looks primarily at the underlying psychological issues leading to addiction such as depression, anxiety and family issues. It also considers the resulting effect on quality of life and exacerbation of the original issues due to the addiction (i.e., greater depression, suicidality, psychosis).

Ultimately, what determines whether someone is addicted to a substance is whether or not they are able to stop using without any consequences such as withdrawal, or delirium tremens. Has their quality of life diminished to such a degree that it affects relationships with family or friends adversely, or that they are unable to function at work or in the home? If so, they may be addicted.

Understanding these addiction fundamentals is your key to dealing with addicted Toxic Clients.

Case No. 13: The CPA

Victor Lee had recently hired a new receptionist, Susan Wright, for his growing Seattle CPA practice. Susan was a very pleasant lady in her mid-twenties. She had just moved from a small town in central Washington to the Emerald City and was wide eyed by the big city.

Shortly after she started Susan took a call from a very nice man named Tyler. She listened intently as Tyler explained his situation in great detail. His wife had abruptly left him and Susan felt awful for what Tyler had just been though. Tyler said he needed help preparing his taxes and wondered if Mr. Lee could help him given his situation. Susan felt great sympathy for Tyler and agreed to get him an appointment.

When Tyler arrived at the scheduled time Susan smelled a slight whiff of alcohol on his breath.

His eyes were bloodshot and his clothes disheveled. He was not the nice man she had imagined on the phone. As she showed Tyler into Mr. Lee's office she felt a sense of unease.

Victor and Tyler's discussion went on for 10 minutes before the shouting started. Victor threw open the door and demanded that Tyler leave. Tyler left the office in a loud and hostile manner. Victor locked the door behind him and sat down in front of Susan. He took a deep, calming breath.

"Have you ever heard of the word naiveté?" he asked Susan.

"Yes. I believe so," she meekly responded.

"What does it mean?" Victor asked evenly.

"Being too trusting. Too innocent."

"Exactly right, and we have to ban naiveté from this office."

Susan nodded as Victor went on to explain what happened. Tyler had told him the tale of woe. The same concocted story he had told Susan on the phone. Victor had learned to actively listen to his new clients. He interpreted and evaluated what they said. In this case, it was all a ruse for Victor to do Tyler's taxes for free.

Susan was taken back. People didn't do that where she came from.

Victor said they probably did. There were addicts everywhere now.

Susan still didn't understand why he wanted free CPA services.

Victor explained that drug and alcohol abusers needed to feed their addiction. If they could get free CPA services with a tale of woe, the money they would have spent on a tax return could be "better" used for more drugs and alcohol. Due to their dependency they would tell falsehoods to family, friends, vendors and anyone else within the economic cycle. They would say anything to anyone to stay medicated.

Victor was still angered by Tyler's sense of entitlement. As Victor was not swayed by the tale of woe, Tyler had then switched to the argument that since Victor made enough money doing tax returns he owed a person with needs like Tyler a complimentary service. Tyler stressed that Victor had a societal responsibility, which meant doing free work for the less fortunate.

It was when Victor said, "You mean doing free work for alcoholics," that the shouting started.

Susan now understood. She had seen the street people in Seattle. She was initially shocked but now sadly used to it. These types were easy to identify. But addicts came in all forms. And they told all forms of lies to fuel their dependency. She was resolved to be less trusting.

Lesson #7: Toxic Clients prey on the naïve. Ban naiveté from your office.

Case No. 14: The Carpet Cleaner

Ruben Blanco owned a prosperous carpet cleaning company. His company operated three vans filled with expensive cleaning equipment that traveled to people's homes and removed stains and discolorations from their carpets. It was a good business that came with one big issue. If you did work inside or around people's houses you had to deal with the neuroses individuals had about their private, personal property. This issue was only compounded when dealing with an addict.

Elijah Anderson was a successful businessman in his 40's. He had a very nice house in a very nice neighborhood. Elijah had recently thrown a party where some red wine had been spilled on the carpet. Ruben loved that people were drinking more red wine at parties. More wine, more spills, more carpet cleaning. As he joked with his friends, "Business is grape!"

When Ruben arrived at Elijah's house he was stunned at the extent of the damage. It was not just a spill here and there. There were spills everywhere, as if there had been massive Malbec food fight. There was red wine on the walls and the ceilings in addition to all over the carpets and furniture.

"Quite a party" Ruben said dryly. Elijah shrugged. "It was fun then."

Ruben explained that he could clean the carpets and could attempt to do the furniture. He stated that he would not be able to clean the walls and the ceiling.

Elijah said he understood. He said he had another gathering planned and would like it cleaned within a week. Elijah said he would be on a business trip for the next three days. He encouraged them to clean in his absence. Ruben agreed that they would do their best, and his crew started to work.

It was the biggest residential job Ruben had ever encountered. Not only were the living room, kitchen and family areas soiled, but every bedroom, bathroom and closet had red wine markings. Ruben and his crew actively wondered:

"What kind of party was this?"

On the floor of an upstairs closet underneath a tiny black cocktail dress one of the workers found what appeared to be a large bag of cocaine. Ruben was called to survey the scene. Should they flush it down the toilet? Ruben wasn't sure it was cocaine. The crew laughed and one said there was an easy way to tell. Ruben was against that and decided that no one's fingerprints should be on the bag. Using gloves they placed the dress and the bag on a shelf above and cleaned the closet floor.

Elijah returned three days later, entered his house and was furious. They had not touched the ceiling or the walls. The job wasn't finished and he had friends coming over that night.

Ruben was firm. He had specifically said he could not clean the ceilings and walls. He reminded Elijah that he said he needed just the carpets cleaned in a week, not three days.

Elijah exploded. He yelled that he needed the entire job done in three days. They hadn't done it so they weren't getting paid!

Ruben and the other workers clearly noticed Elijah's glassy eyes and sniffling nose. He was on cocaine right then. He was self-righteous and grandiose in his blaming of Ruben and the crew. Elijah shouted that he knew that a pathetic Mom and Pop shop wouldn't get the job done as he specifically requested.

Ruben stood his ground. He would not be blamed. He was clear on the service he could offer and the time in which it could be performed. He spoke in a firm and yet calm voice as Elijah's voice grew ever louder.

Ruben knew not to match Elijah's anger with his own. That would only add fuel to the fire.

Elijah swore that he would write a scathing and brutal online review at Yelp and all the other sites about their horrible and unprofessional service if they didn't leave right then. He screamed that they needed to immediately get off his property or he would call the police.

Ruben said they weren't going to flush the fees they had earned down the toilet. At this the rest of the crew laughed, which temporarily broke the tension.

Another worker then said, "Yeah, if you call the police there's a bag of white powder we'd like to show them."

Elijah was enraged the entire time he wrote out the check for their services. He angrily huffed that hideous online reviews were headed their way. Ruben took the check. He and the crew gladly left.

When dealing with addicts do not allow yourself to be sucked into the blame game. If you did not create the problem never allow yourself to be blamed for it. As well, being polite and/

or skirting the issue may not serve you well. While you don't want to get angry yourself, or match their level of anger, you must also be firm and extremely clear on what happened. Do not accept the addict's version of events. Addicts will probe for weakness, shadings and small concessions. They will recite 'facts' to make it seem as if you did something wrong, a fee-goading technique used to gain leverage and a discount. There must be no room for such interpretations. You cannot yield to their manipulations. You must be frank and direct about every-thing. You must tell it as it is and demand to be paid.

Addicts and other Toxic Clients will threaten you with bad reviews if you do not do what they want. You must be blithe-ly unconcerned about such intimidations. He who cares least wins. A person who says they are going to write a bad review is going to do so anyway, whether you accommodate them or not. So don't give in to their loud ultimatums.

You may want to let the client know that a threat of bad reviews is a form of extortion. You could honestly state that people have gone to jail for extortion. (Which they have, but not yet from threats of bad reviews. But there is a good chance the other guy doesn't know that.)

On the other hand, you may not even care at all. I believe most people take online reviews with a grain of salt, or even a salt mine or two. They now know that some glowing reviews are written by friends and the nasty ones are written by com-petitors or toxic persons. Where is the truth in an online review?

A friend of mine is a podiatrist. She has three zero star re-views on Yelp, which out of six reviews really drags down her score. If you read the negative reviews the complaints are all because the upset reviewer couldn't get into see her for six or seven weeks. She is professional, well respected, and busy and in the twisted logic of the day she received negative reviews for being professional, well respected and busy.

However, there can be benefits to negative reviews. A recent survey found that three quarters of all customers trust sites that post negative reviews, and 95% of unhappy customers will return if issues can be resolved. If you publicly respond mistakes and problems and learn from them you can turn the negatives into positives. Not everyone is a Toxic Client.

When dealing with those suffering from alcohol and drug abuse, remember active listening. If you listen carefully these troubled types will clearly present themselves. In Case No. 14: The Carpet Cleaner, Ruben Blanco noticed all the signs of drug use, and stood his ground against the attempted manipulations of cocaine user Elijah Anderson. In Case No. 13: The CPA, Victor Lee actively listened to learn that Tyler was an alcoholic with entitlement issues. It is best to avoid these types altogether, rather than become intertwined in their issues.

There are now a large number of people in the marketplace who suffer from alcohol and drug issues. Be ready for them. And if need be, be ready to show them the door.

Chapter Eight:

Entitlementia

"Man is not, by nature, deserving of all that he wants. When we think we are entitled to something, that is when we start walking all over others to get it."
~Criss Jami

In October of 2009, a woman emerged from a stretch limousine and entered the Burlington Coat Factory in Columbus, Ohio. She made a grand announcement to the store's customers. Having just won the lottery she was going to buy everyone a present of up to $500 in merchandise.

The store lit up. Customers called friends and family to come down right now for free clothes. Soon 500 people filled the aisles and flooded the register lines. Another 1,000 people were outside pushing to get in.

However, the women hadn't won the lottery. Without paying for anything she got back into the limo and left.

When customers learned that they weren't getting their free stuff a riot erupted. Even though the promise turned out to be false the customers still felt entitled to the free clothing. In a frenzy clothes were pulled off the shelves and stolen. The sense of entitlement led to a collective agitation and hysteria.

When people slip into the entitlement mentality bad things can happen. On a small scale, you will have to deal with more Toxic Clients. On a larger scale, nations can fall. Citizens with an entitlement mentality are growing in numbers. While a social safety net is important, those who expect you to facilitate their entitled lifestyle must be understood and dealt with.

The entitlement mentality is a form of dementia, hence the term Entitlementia. Dementia isn't any one disease. Rather it is a bundle of symptoms affecting one's thinking and social abilities enough to interfere with normal living. Signs of dementia include a difficulty with planning and organizing, an inability to reason, inappropriate behavior, a decrease in motivation and problems with memory. When those with dementia are placed in situations beyond their abilities, they often react with anger, frustration and an eruption of emotion. The most common form of dementia is Alzheimer's disease, which makes up 55% to 65% of all cases. Many of us have known or dealt with a person afflicted by Alzheimer's. An entitlement mentality also displays the same core characteristics of dementia. They can often lack motivation, have impaired social skills, exhibit improper behavior and agitation, and have difficulty remembering things or remembering them correctly.

Psychologists view entitlement as a continuum of personality traits that range from the less severe self-absorption all the way to narcissism.

While they all involve a perspective in which selfish needs dominate over empathy and sacrifice, the degree of severity will affect how you interact with and manage these people. Righteousness, grandiosity, and self- centeredness are other terms to describe the characteristics of these individuals.

At the far end of the continuum is a disorder we mentioned in a previous chapter, Narcissistic Personality Disorder (NPD). Those with NPD have an obsessive need for attention and admiration, an amplified sense of self-importance as well as a strong sense of entitlement. In believing they are superior they have little time or patience for the feelings of others. Indeed, they view people as simple objects to fulfill their needs, and will use any tactic without remorse to get what they want. Narcissist Victim Abuse describes the children, spouses and peers affected by such aberrant behavior.

Entitlementia is found in all demographic groups. Numerous sources have put forth that affluenza (a combination of the words affluence and influenza) is a form of Entitlement. The presence of or a great desire for wealth, it is posited, leads to depression, neglect of personal relationships, an inability to delay gratification and a false sense of entitlement. The blind pursuit of money can leave some blind to everything else that is important.

How do people become entitled? Are our brains "hardwired," genetically predisposed to being narcissistic? The answer is "Yes."

Entitlement is a normal stage of development in children and adolescents and is the way their rudimentary communication tells the world their wants and needs. They haven't yet developed an understanding of how their wants and needs may get in the way of other's wants and needs. As we mature, we learn the nuances of these complex interactions and interplays. Unfortunately, there are some who, for whatever reason, don't grow out of that phase and continue to view the world from their self-centered perspective. Their cravings are more important than anyone else's realistic needs. Over time their condition sets in as Entitlementia.

What does it mean to have a sense of entitlement? Such an individual will:

- Impose unrealistic demands on their family, friends, acquaintances, employees and/or employers.

- See that their needs come first, even if it means inconveniencing others. Making people wait, taking the last piece of food or cancelling appointments without regard for others are all examples.
- They see rules that apply to others don't apply to them. Cutting in line because they are late is just fine. But no one should dare cut in front of them.
- Asking for favors from others is not a big deal, but when others ask them for a favor it is a major burden.
- The things they are interested in are much more important than other peoples' interests.
- They resent it when others don't give them special treatment. When buying a car, they expect a price well below cost. When they don't get it, they are angry and resentful. However, when they are making money, they expect to get top dollar from everyone else.
- They confuse the pursuit of happiness with a right to happiness, which no one deserves more than they do.
- They focus on other peoples' flaws, but when theirs are pointed out, they get angry.
- They frequently talk about their rights.
- Memories of past events can be distorted to fit their view of superiority over others.

Both Entitlementia and NPD are not often diagnosed. (If it were those affected would feel entitled to treatment.) With such individuals going undetected in society and with more and more individuals environmentally conditioned to possess such qualities, society itself moves toward a collective pattern of unhealthy thoughts and behaviors.

A problem of Entitlementia has to do with a severing of the link between actions and consequences. Government programs are administered solely on need, with both political parties seeking favor by identifying more needs. But the causes of such needs, including the choices people have made, are not a factor in the giving. Thus there is no effort to even identify, much less correct, the problems. As well, when recipients owe nothing – not even gratitude – normal human behaviors and motivations are skewed. With a steady diet of entitlement the individual loses his or her ability for executive function and problem solving. People are conditioned to a state of learned helplessness. They adapt to the expectation of receiving rather than achieving. From CEO's and Senators and on down the line, they act like selfish and spoiled children when any mention of reducing what they think they are entitled to is discussed.

So how do you deal with Toxic Clients displaying the signs of Entitlementia?

First try and understand their agenda. Is it trying to get the best deal, shirking the rules or inflating their sense of superiority?

Car salesmen are usually very good judges of character. They see all types. A friend named Eric South sells Ford pickups and passenger cars. He states that everyone wants the best deal. He is used to that. The entitled, the self-important, however, want to break all the dealership rules and come away with a lopsided winning transaction in their very great favor. They must win without regard for the basics of the business — making a profit to keep the doors open. They are entitled to the best deal because they are simply better than everyone else.

Eric finds such customers so unrealistic in their demands and so time-consuming to deal with that he just points to the Chevy dealership down the street. Eric has learned to avoid such individuals. His sales manager agrees. Understanding the client's agenda early on and sending them on their way early on is best for the dealership. Eric admits that if such customers do come back they end up paying more for a car than they would have initially. The dealership believes in PITA pricing (or "Pain in the Ass" pricing, discussed ahead.)

The entitled are often of the belief that they should not have to pay for anything. You will hear people claim that all music, movies and writings should come at no cost. They will feel no guilt in illegally downloading musicians', filmmakers' and authors' work for free. In doing so they have stolen from the artist (and raised the price for everyone else.) But their Entitlementia blindly places their immediate needs ahead of any crime or consequence.

Know that Entitlementia may start in small doses, like illegal downloads. But as it grows, you as the business owner must stand firm against it.

Case No. 15: The Insurance Agency

Liz worked for a local American Family Insurance agency. Her job was to remind existing auto insurance clients that their premiums were due. She would phone and email them at least five times to notify them that if payment was not received their policy would be canceled.

Of course, when the policies lapsed for non-payment a number of people would barge into the agency screaming and yelling with indignation, "How dare you cancel my policy!"

"You didn't pay on time," Liz would calmly respond.

"No one told me that!"

"I have a record of five phone calls and emails," Liz would reply.

"I demand that you reinstate the policy right now!"

Liz would ask: "Do you have money for the new policy?"

"No. I want the old policy renewed and I want you to pay the premium!"

"Why should we pay the premium?"

"Because you let it lapse!"

"No we didn't. It is your responsibility to pay on time."

"I am entitled to that policy and you need to make the payment."

"It is against state law for us to pay a client's premium."

"Well, that is a stupid state law. You need to pay my premium and renew my policy right now!"

Liz would smile and say: "Why should we lose our insurance license for you?"

"Because I need insurance and you lost it for me!"

"Do you recall any of the messages left for you to pay on time?"

"Of course not, I'm too busy. You need to make this right. I demand that you pay my premium!"

At some point Liz would pick up the phone and say "Code 7."

Within the agency Code 7 meant an unruly customer. A manager would come out and try to deal with the person. They would encourage the irate person to calm down. They would encourage them to talk in the conference room, away from the other customers in the reception area. In some cases, the customer could be talked down. In others, the customer didn't have the money and would leave without insurance. In a few cases it went to "Code 9" and the police were called.

It is important to have a procedure within the office for dealing with unruly and angry clients. Even if you have never faced such a client before it makes sense to be well prepared for the first one. Some offices place a buzzer under the reception desk. When pressed, the managers know to come forward. If that tactic isn't used a code word is the next best thing. Developing a Code 7 and Code 9 procedure ahead of a problem can save a lot of time and anxiety when the problem is suddenly in front of you. Get creative with your cipher. Your code may be "Paging Mr. Dangerfield" or "The Raiders are playing." Just be sure that it is a code that everyone can remember and that all new hires learn about it as part of their job training.

In college my friends and I had a code word for trouble. If there was a fight or one of our guys was getting into a bad spot we all knew to call out the word. And we all knew to respond immediately if the word was called. We only had to use it once during those four years, and it worked like a charm. With a show of force, the escalating problem was promptly de-escalated.

Lesson #8: Have an established procedure for dealing with angry and unruly clients.

A client with Entitlementia can be very frustrating. You work hard to keep the doors open. They could care less. They are entitled to your time and services, without regard for normal commerce. As with alcohol and drug abusers, sometimes the only way to handle them is to show them the door.

Chapter Nine:

Tar Babies

"If you think there's a solution, you're part of the problem."
~ George Carlin

The term "tar baby" comes from a story in the Uncle Remus tales written by Joel Chandler Harris in 1881. The story, called "The Wonderful Tar Baby Story," is about the trickster Brer Rabbit, who has always eluded capture by the hungry Brer Fox. Brer Fox sets a trap for the wily rabbit by making a "baby" out of tar and turpentine, and dressing it up like a little boy. When Brer Rabbit comes wandering by, he stops to say hello to the tar baby, but of course gets no response. The baby's lack of response eventually frustrates Brer Rabbit so much that he taps the baby, and becomes inextricably caught in the mess of tar. The harder he fights and more punches he swings, the more deeply stuck he is in the tar.

Though interpretations over the last century have widely differed, with many associating the concept of a "tar baby" with a racial slur, the concept is often used in business and psychotherapy to mean, "a client with so many troubles that the more you try to get out of them, the deeper into them you sink." These are clients that try to drag us into their problems and bind us up in the drama that accompanies them. And they're often so good at manipulating us (they've honed it all their lives) that we come right along with them into Drama Town, realizing only too late that we're stuck in the muck with them. In other words, tar babies are drama hounds.

That drama often comes from nowhere. Like Brer Rabbit, who was unassumingly strolling along, minding his own business, when he came upon a stranger and innocently said hello, business owners frequently can't see the trouble of a tar baby, even when it's staring them in the face. And by the time they begin to engage with the client, it's too late to get out.

Case No. 16: The HVAC Owner

Karl Richards owned a prosperous HVAC business. He knew heating, venting and air conditioning like no other. And Karl made sure his employees also knew the trade inside and out. When a customer was freezing for lack of heat or roasting for an absence of air conditioning you needed to respond and fix quickly.

One of Karl's very first clients was Jimmy Zolezzi. His firm was one of the largest property managers in the area. Zolezzi and his team managed single home rentals for small investors, large apartment complexes for pension funds and all the duplexes and 8 plexes in between. When Karl left his original employer to start his own HVAC firm, Zolezzi sent all his property management work to Karl's new firm, which had made all the difference for the start up. As a result, Karl had a soft spot for Zolezzi, who had provided a shot in the arm when Karl needed it most.

The two had become friends through the years, and Zolezzi would often call to vent about clients that the two were doing work for. Most of the time, Karl didn't charge for the time spent on such phone calls, since they weren't always work-related. But occasionally, Karl did bill for such calls, if they were actively discussing client projects.

Because of the friendship that had developed between them, and because Zolezzi seemed to have taken on a sort of mentor role with Karl, Zolezzi would often balk at the bills Karl sent him for various jobs, telling him that he was too inexperienced and was taking way too long to do certain jobs. He'd question the number of hours Karl had spent, and say things like, "All I asked you to do was change a setting. That should only have taken you 15 minutes, tops!" or "I can't believe you charge for phone calls. I never do that. That's just the cost of doing business!" Karl tended to take such discussions in stride. The paying work Zolezzi sent his way was still, all in all, productive for Karl.

Zolezzi then went through a terrible and acrimonious divorce. Everyone in town gossiped about it. A cute young intern became pregnant, the rumors pointed to Zolezzi as the father and Zolezzi's wife was publicly mortified. Her bitterness knew no end. Of the couple's many friends, all sided with her. Zolezzi was adrift.

Since Karl was not socially friendly with Zolezzi and his wife, he couldn't really choose sides based on just rumors. Karl only knew Zolezzi. Which meant Zolezzi would call to talk about a lot more than business. Zolezzi would talk about the wrath of his ex, the superficiality of their friends (some of whom Karl knew quite well) who sided with her and the loss, account by account, asset by asset, of his hard-earned personal wealth.

The loss of this wealth put a huge strain of Zolezzi's business. Zolezzi now looked to cut every corner he could. When calling to vent with Karl about his demonic divorce Zolezzi would also try to whittle down any HVAC bills Karl had submitted. "My clients can't afford your bills," he would say and, "I can't afford to lose another client."

Karl became very uncomfortable with the evolving, now toxic relationship. He recognized that he should be grateful for everything Zolezzi had done to help him get started. Zolezzi had made a huge difference at a crucial stage. But that was many years ago. And while over the years Karl would grant Zolezzi a discount here and there, now Zolezzi expected a 'friend discount' for every bit of work Karl performed.

As well, Zolezzi was taking up many hours of Karl's productive time to talk about a divorce that was anything but productive. Karl felt very awkward learning about Zolezzi's declining financial situation and the former inner workings and dysfunction of a now very failed marriage. Karl preferred boundaries and grew very frustrated that Zolezzi crossed them every day, which incursions kept Karl from more gainful activities himself. Karl knew he had a business to run, and that Zolezzi's calls and complaints were preventing him from running it.

One day, Karl was talking to Jason McMahon, a real estate investor he had met professionally through Zolezzi. A comment by McMahon really struck him. The investor said the best thing he had ever done was side with Zolezzi's wife in the divorce. Up until that point Zolezzi would call him all the time and dump on him about his problems. McMahon said he had wasted hours and hours listening to Zolezzi. McMahon said someone else must have started listening, and he was grateful for that.

With that, Karl finally decided the boundaries had to be set.

The next day when Zolezzi called, he didn't take it. Another five calls came in that day from Zolezzi. Karl did not return one of them. By the end of the day Karl felt refreshed. He had gotten more work done than he had in three months.

The next day Karl received several emails from Zolezzi. One of them was about repairing an AC unit at a 4-plex in the middle of town. While Karl always wanted more work, he realized that he would be nickel-and-dimed on every item of the charge. Karl sent a polite email back saying they were too busy to get to it that week.

Zolezzi took a while to get the hint, and for weeks sent Karl more long, personal email messages detailing how difficult things were for him—his clients were too demanding, his ex had just launched another attack on his assets, he didn't have the money to do anything anymore. Karl had to be very strict with himself and not get embroiled in Zolezzi's drama. It was clear to see that Zolezzi was lonely and needed a friend, but Karl needed to protect himself and his business from such a drain on his energy, time and finances. While Karl tried to be candid and straight forward in all his dealings, in this case he felt avoidance was the best choice. Talking through problems didn't work when all the other side wanted to do was to talk. It was like trying to stop a flood by adding more water.

Eventually, Zolezzi stopped contacting Karl and found another HVAC firm. Although Karl was sad to lose Zolezzi's friendship and the work Zolezzi's firm brought to him, he is pleased to see how much more work he's getting done these days.

Jimmy Zolezzi is a tar baby. He has so many problems that the relationship with Karl had turned from mutually beneficial to a singular crutch. Unless you are a psychologist or counselor, you are not in the business of serving as someone else's crutch. You cannot afford to serve in that role for several reasons:

- A tar baby sucks prime time from your work day.

- A tar baby will frequently discuss money issues, and look to you for 'friendly discounts' to a complete financial rescue.

- A tar baby will talk for as long as you listen, meaning they will set no boundaries on your time.

- A tar baby will drain your energy as long as you allow them to do so.

A key issue for the tar baby is to have someone who will listen. As you phase out of that role please be certain they will be finding someone else to dump on. You may feel guilty when setting the boundaries and/or avoiding their contact, guilty that you are not taking their call in a time of need. But that guilt will dissipate once you are clear from them and sense that they have found another person to fill that role, at which point you will realize that you were not really that special to the tar baby at all. Instead, you were just the latest in the long line of people willing to pick up the phone and listen.

There is not much you can do for such a client. As we've discussed, you can express empathy and understanding for what that person is experiencing, and that makes a big difference in defusing heightened emotions. But you also have to remember that it isn't your problem—it's theirs. You have to remain detached if you're going to get away from a tar baby.

Lesson #9: Be rubber, not glue. Don't let Toxic Clients' problems stick to you.

It might also help to remember that for some people, drama will always be a constant presence. These are the people you talk to who always have terrible things going on in their lives. Every day is the worst, every argument is a huge fight, every person they know is out to get them, every health problem is a nail in the coffin … The truth is that they enjoy that drama, they seek it out. That drama keeps the attention focused on them. Giving them the attention they crave only feeds the swirl of drama that surrounds them, and it will pull you down in its wake if you let it.

Tar babies can pull you in like a black hole. Just as a great amount of compressed matter in space can have a pull so strong that not even light can escape, so can a tar baby suck you into their darkness. The closer you get the harder it may be to escape.

I had such a client recently. She set up a consult with the office to discuss 'asset protection and taxes.' That is a standard discussion I have with clients, so no red flags there. But when she got on the phone her issues were anything but standard. After half an hour of a tale of woe she came to the point. She wanted advice on how to cheat the IRS.

I politely explained that I assist clients to legally minimize their taxes. It is called tax avoidance. But to evade taxes, as she wanted to do, was illegal. I told her the old joke that the difference between tax avoidance and tax evasion was 20 years. (In prison.)

But she was adamant. She had read a lot of information on the internet that said by using the right attorney and their trust account one wouldn't ever have to pay taxes. I explained that the terms 'internet' and 'information' were frequently mutually exclusive. At this point she became shrill, insisting I must not be a very experienced lawyer in this area.

With humor not working on her and certainly appropriate, I suggested she "call Saul." She was immediately interested in the name of an attorney who could help. I had to explain I was referring to the fictional Saul Goodman, the 'criminal' criminal attorney on the TV show 'Breaking Bad' (whose popularity has led to his spin-off). She was furious. She insisted that there were actual attorneys who help people avoid the unconstitutional reach of the IRS. I politely explained I was not such an attorney and ended the call.

She called the office the next day. She was still angry. She demanded a full refund of her consultation fee. She said I gave her no advice on how to cheat the IRS.

Let's stop right here and analyze this person. She is clearly a Toxic Client. She has no clue as to the ethical obligations of attorneys. She doesn't want to know them. She has her strange orbit and you must submit to it. Or not. Don't let a self-centered black hole client suck you into their manic vortex. You must avoid these people.

Of course we gave her a refund. I wanted nothing to do with her.

She was the kind of person who would post scathing, negative online reviews. While you can't let your business be governed by such threats it helps when you can at least respond. Due to attorney/client privilege restraints, I would not be able to answer back: "She wanted me to help her cheat the IRS!" As an attorney it is nearly impossible to defend yourself in such a situation. Besides, who has the time or energy for that? Give them a refund and send them on their way.

Remember the Pareto Principle, or the 80/20 rule. Tar babies are the 20 percent of your income taking up the 80 percent of your time. If you are to be successful in business, you'll need to focus your energy on those 20 percent of your clients that produce 80 percent of your revenue. Stay away from tar babies.

Chapter Ten:

Identify

"Everything yields to diligence."
~ Antiphanes

It is important to be able to identify Toxic Clients. But first you must make sure the problem wasn't of your own doing at the outset. I learned this the hard way.

In Chapter One I mentioned my father was an Alameda County Superior Court Judge in Oakland, California. In Chapter Four I discussed working as a young waiter who spoke first and thought second in Washington D.C. In this case the two storylines intersected.

My father's best friend on the bench, a smart judge who appreciated a good joke, came into the Georgetown restaurant where I worked. He brought with him another D.A. friend who had just been appointed to a high government office. (A number of lawyers who worked in the Alameda County District Attorney's Office were appointed to significant federal jobs during the Reagan Administration.)

After pleasantries I set about to take their order. But the political appointee was scowling at me. He definitely was not happy. It made me very uncomfortable.

The French owner was not working that day. In his place was the French manager, who was the most suave individual I have ever met. He could talk cats out of trees. He was even better with customers. When I mentioned my discomfort he immediately focused on what I may have done to make the customer unhappy. I said that I met the man for the first time, told a little joke and set about taking their drink order. I couldn't imagine why the man was so grim.

The manager forced me to elaborate. So I replayed the whole scene. My father's friend introduced me to the man who has just been appointed the head of the U.S. Immigration and Naturalization Service. I laughed and said not to go back in the kitchen and that was it.

The manager stopped me right there. "You just met the head of U.S. Immigration for the first time and the very first thing you said to him was: Don't go back in the kitchen?!"

Before he could say "You idiot!" I interrupted him. "You told me everyone back there was legal."

He paused. "Well…we're not sure about the dishwashers."

Now my joke really was not funny. "Oh great! Now what do we do?"

The French manager had all the polish and sophistication I did not. Hundreds of years earlier, as unruly and insubordinate Huguenots, my entire family had been permanently kicked out of France. Suave was not part of our makeup.

But the French manager knew exactly what to do. He grabbed the largest and nicest bottle of champagne in the restaurant and a sword. He had done this before. With a grand gesture in front of their table and the whole restaurant watching he swiftly ran the sword up the neck of the bottle. When the sword hit the bottle's rim the cork went flying in the air, champagne came foaming out and glasses were filled. The entire restaurant was impressed. The manager toasted his new friends, and several glasses of soothing bubbly were consumed. By the end of the meal, along with complimentary desserts, the judge and the head of the U.S. Immigration were in a happy mood.

The manager deducted the bottle of champagne and the free desserts from my paycheck. I deserved it, and learned a good lesson. My job was not to make a joke for the benefit of one customer at the expense of the other; my job was to make both customers feel welcome.

When dealing with Toxic Clients you have to first ask yourself if you have done anything to create the problem. I certainly had.

In your situation, did an employee say something to set off the customer? Was an order improperly handled at the start? Were unrealistically high expectations set at the very beginning?

You must first be very candid with yourself and the facts. Toxic Clients are not self-aware. They don't 'see' their behavior as inappropriate. As such, you must be all the more aware. If you or your staff created the problem you must tailor your response. Just as the French manager made the two diners feel extra special that night, you may have to go a bit further just to bring things back into equilibrium.

Once that review is completed you may determine that you did nothing wrong. This is very useful and will guide your approach.

But how do we identify Toxic Clients at the start? It can be very difficult.

It is not always easy to tell who is or is not toxic until a business relationship has taken a serious turn for the worse. On the plus side, the more experience you gain from being in business, the easier it will be to identify a Toxic Client. Still, even longtime business owners can be caught off guard. One reason for this is that, to some extent, being a business owner means being a bit of an optimist. You must expect success in delivering goods or services to satisfied customers, or you wouldn't be willing to try it at all.

Frank Troppe is a sales and management expert and author of two books who consults for sales organizations around the country. Frank notes: "Not many customers look toxic at the outset, so it's easy to get lulled into a sense of complacency because we want to believe the best is going to happen. Whether we're in a small business or a large enterprise, one wealth lever is to focus our optimism only on those people we can help the most."

The unfortunate truth is that Toxic Clients have a way of sneaking up on us and infecting us with their toxicity before we even detect the symptoms. Even savvy, experienced business owners can fall victim.

That's why it's so important to practice identifying the signs of Toxic Clients before we ever do business with them.

Here are the most common identifying marks of toxicity to be found in clients:

- Asking for or expecting free advice
- Not paying, or manipulating the payment process— negotiating for discounts, trade-outs, credit, or other non-standard arrangements
- Missing appointments or deadlines
- Making impossible demands
- Being abusive
- Acting irrationally
- Not making good use of your services

This chapter is designed to show you some of the most common signs of toxicity. Work on using the strategies presented so that you can immediately identify these behaviors and develop a resistance to them.

Clients who want free advice

As an attorney, I used to face this issue. I would receive phone calls from people who'd present legal scenarios to me and ask for my opinion about how they should proceed. They were often looking for fast, free advice on a matter, but didn't intend to hire me. Now, we have a receptionist screening calls. Unless it's my wife or kids, you don't get through without a booked appointment.

The same thing happens to me in social situations. At a party, I might be asked what I think about some legal problem someone's having. After years of practicing law, I know that a small amount of this is to be expected, and with good friends I am happy to listen. But with new acquaintances, I have learned to draw firm boundaries and not overly engage in such discussions. Anyone willing to spill out personal and confidential information in the midst of a very social gathering is someone who should be reigned in by suggesting that an in-office consultation is the more appropriate venue. I am very thankful if they do not call since, chances are, they were toxic to begin with. Over the years I have, as will you, become good at identifying this sign of a future problem customer and steer clear of it.

Frank Troppe has been a sales consultant for decades. But despite expertise in his field developed over many years, he had to learn some important lessons after he went into business for himself. And one of the most important lessons was that some potential clients were only interested in picking his brain.

"When I started our firm," says Troppe, "we were willing to talk to anybody. What I soon came to realize was that we were having meetings at which people were not really interested in budgeting for an engagement. They just wanted free advice. This happens all the time in my field. 'Thanks for the information, but we'll try and do it ourselves.'" (For a humorous reenactment of these kinds of situations search YouTube for The Vendor-Client Relationship.)

Managers with an employee-staffing company, in fact, burned up two separate two-hour meetings with Troppe, who had spent an additional four hours apiece preparing for each meeting. The 12 hours he lost weren't the end of it, either. The meetings were followed by subsequent phone calls that totaled another two hours. The managers never hired Troppe.

Live and learn.

"It was my fault," Troppe says. "I should have laid out terms of the engagement in our first meeting. In the consulting business, this can happen pretty easily and requires discipline on the part of the consultant to say 'no' at certain points in the sales process. We learned from this experience to close the sale on paid engagements early in the process—including requiring that the client will pay for our analysis."

After several years in business for himself, and having built a solid track record, Troppe has become more selective about whom he'll consider as a prospect. And he considers his time valuable, and to be paid for, during the screening process.

"I'll meet once with anyone who looks like a qualified client," Troppe says. "I often get a fee up front for initial consultations. Or at the minimum, I'll have my expenses, such as research and out-of-town travel, covered."

Troppe has extensive experience in coaching managers and sales forces. Before becoming a consultant, he earned a law degree and spent 15 years managing field operations himself for various companies. He is a certified facilitator for Miller Heiman—the worldwide company well known for its innovations in the sales-training industry.

But being in business for oneself involves the extra challenge of scrupulous time management—especially while marketing one's services.

"Anybody with a small consulting firm will have to be disciplined in the time he or she spends selling to prospective clients," Troppe says.

"You can get people to talk about their problems all day long, but it doesn't make you any money—or, in the end, the client any money—if all you're doing is talking."

After several years of running the Branch Productivity Institute, Troppe has developed profiles of "standard engagements" with good clients. These are the relationships he pursues with new clients. Troppe also has learned to watch for several warning signs when screening prospects, including:

- Lack of a budget to pay for services.
- Not openly sharing business goals. This implies that the client isn't envisioning a long-term relationship. "It means you're viewed only as a commodity provider, not a specialist," Troppe says.
- Appearing only to be interested in a one-time, low-level engagement, such as a speech or seminar, regardless of the outcome. "They're seeking a flavor-of-the-month program for their company," Troppe says. "That for us is good for short-term cash flow, but in the long run it's not the kind of business we want to build. We're less interested in short-term gratification and more interested in long-term growth for a client. Then we can point to a track record of success."
- Asking for payment terms that diverge significantly from Troppe's standards: net upon receipt for speeches or seminars; 30-day net for retained services. "If somebody

says, 'Let's wait for six months and see what the results are,' that's a no-go unless we've also contracted for gain —sharing at the end of those six months."

Troppe always keeps an eye out for clients deliberately— or even unintentionally—using his expertise without paying for it.

Not paying

Not paying on time is always a red flag. If the client has agreed to pay the monthly retainer, but is paying invoices 90 or 120 days out, that's a sign worth paying attention to.

"Usually, people don't come out and say, 'We need four months to pay our bills,'" Troppe says. "But if that's happening, it's already looking like a non-standard engagement."

Troppe's diplomatic term "non-standard" could be said another way: flaky.

A Toxic Client complicates the payment process. His check bounces, he asks for credit, he negotiates for discounts or wants to barter and do a trade-out. Or he lets a balance run seriously overdue. The concept of "no pay, no play" doesn't register with this Toxic Client. And there is no end to the creativity when it comes to covering a bill.

Sometimes, the client will fall into the habit of making a partial payment on an outstanding balance. The client will insist that he or she will have more work coming to you, and then he won't pay the balance until there's another job on the table—a completely different job. You'll be asked to add the outstanding balance to the new order, so despite attempts to appear current, this client is perpetually, strategically, behind.

Sometimes clients bite off more they can chew. They can't afford the goods or services for which they've engaged.

The most common problem clients for contractors are those for whom the work is outside their financial range, says Marvin Washington, the landscape contractor in Case No. 6 who was forced to take the Collingsworths to court for nonpayment.

"They want work done, then when they realize they actually have to pay for it, they get squirrelly," says Washington. "They'll whine, nitpick, and try to get you to cut them a deal for some imagined fault with the work or do additional work for free. They usually just want to pay less than agreed upon."

There are several strategies to employ with this kind of Toxic Client.

"Confronted with this situation," Washington says, "a graphic artist I know very sweetly says, 'Gee, I'm sorry. I didn't realize you couldn't afford this work.' That seems to do the trick."

Appeasement is a second strategy that Washington has used. "It's usually easier than going to court or getting into a pissing match."

He adds, "Sometimes it's good policy if the client is just fussy and hard to please, and it results in return work. You can recoup the expense the next time around. In the end, though, what happens is that our rates increase overall for that client, to cover those instances when you don't get paid for everything you do."

But the best strategy is to avoid these clients in the first place. "Over the years," Washington says, "I've learned to try to ascertain what kind of financial resources people may have. I'm particularly careful with young people who may not have learned to manage their money well.

"With others, I think it's just a bad habit of trying to get something for nothing. I consider it a type of neediness. If I can't appease them, then a letter indicating that I will hand the matter over to my attorney usually takes care of the problem."

Unfortunately, dishonest people exist in our world, people who try to avoid paying their bills altogether. During the process of suing for payment, Washington discovered that the Collingsworths had stiffed a number of contractors. And they may have been playing other financial games.

At one point during that period, a private investigator contacted Washington. He was representing an insurance company that suspected Dexter Collingsworth of filing a false claim on a private unemployment policy. Washington told the private eye that he had met Collingsworth in his office before, but had never seen him actually performing any work.

"These clients made a career of defrauding people who perform work for them, including stiffing the teenage babysitter," Washington says. "It was a perverse game for them. The pains they took to cheat would have exhausted a normal person."

Missing appointments

Your time is valuable. Especially in business, when "time is money." You fill your workday with productive hours. A client who shows up late or stands you up is stealing from you. This is even true if you are able to bill for the missed time or appointment. Why? Because your business' reputation is based on producing results. When a client arrives late or doesn't show up at all, it prevents you from providing goods or services to the client at that time, and therefore to produce results in that time.

Clients who consistently flake on scheduled appointments usually cause waves. They may resist paying (as in Case No. 1:

The Personal Trainer, in which wealthy engineering executive Jeff Kerry kept missing his appointments with fitness trainer Matthew Martinez and refused to pay for the missed sessions). They may blame you or your support staff for the missed appointments.

The bottom line: A client who lacks punctuality lacks respect for you and your business. It is a form of passive hostility. Consider this a big warning sign of toxicity. The time allotted to such a Toxic Client would better be given to a good client.

Lesson #10: Toxic clients don't wear signs announcing themselves. It's your job as a business owner to learn the signs.

Making impossible demands

The Toxic Client is frequently disorganized and needs to be bailed out at the last second. The client often will change an order after the quote or approval of the work, creating further downstream work, and there's always a rush job.

But there are even harsher demands made by Toxic Clients: To be on call 24-7, as if you didn't have other clients as well as a personal life; to fit the client into your schedule no matter who else has been scheduled first; or even to perform magic.

Customers sometimes come to Jenna Starr's salon looking for miracles. She recalls one scenario in which a woman had bleached her hair herself and then re-colored it with products from a supermarket. "It was all crazy, and then she wanted it to match a perfect color in a photograph in a magazine," Starr says. "We told her that it was going to take three or four treatments at the salon to get the hair back to that shiny, beautiful color.

"The hair would have to keep being covered and coated to keep it healthy and to gradually restore the color."

Most clients accept this reality. A few, however, throw a fit after the very first session. Such a client makes a clear point to Starr: "This is a person who can't be pleased. This is a Toxic Client."

Being abusive

Sometimes clients' abuse is subtle, such as when ad director Pauly tried to undermine and sabotage designer Marla Welch. Sometimes the abuse is overt, shaming, and hostile. Examples of this include the woman who called the dermatologist's office and screamed insults at office manager Kenny Adams (Case No. 3: The Dermatologist) when he couldn't get her in immediately for an appointment. Or when George Stinson yelled at Gerald Westerbrook (Case No. 5: The Financial Planner) when his investment returns weren't what he thought they should be.

All such abuse is sending the same message: The client does not respect or value you. And that is not an indicator of a healthy business relationship—either short-term or long-term.

Gerald Westerbrook has a straightforward, decisive policy for handling abusive clients:

"The first time that the client treats me or my staff with disrespect—I don't care how big or how small the client is—our relationship is over. Because our business is all about trust and respect. If clients don't trust me and my professional opinions, and don't respect me and the people who work for me, what do they need me for?"

This is the rule in our office. We have people who are nasty to the receptionist but then very calm and pleasant to me. We call these clients 'Eddie Haskells' after the character in the classic 60's TV show 'Leave It to Beaver.' Eddie would be downright nasty to his friend's younger brother, Beaver Cleaver. But then when Mrs. Cleaver showed up he was nice and charming, to an almost oily degree. We don't tolerate the Eddie Haskells who are nice to the boss but mean to the rest. If you are mean and abusive to even one member of our staff you are toxic. You can find another firm.

Unlike other scenarios, a client's propensity to be abusive is often easy to spot. Heed your common sense and you can detect this warning sign with ease.

And a final warning: "If someone greets you with a drink in hand at 2 o'clock in the afternoon, run like hell," landscape contractor Marvin Washington says. "Drunks are extremely unreasonable."

Not making good use of your services

Sometimes this is a difficult form of toxicity to detect, especially if a client is non-toxic in key areas. The client may be keeping current on your invoices and may be pleasant enough to work with. He or she may be showing up right on time for each and every appointment.

The problem is that the client isn't making use of the services you provide, or considering the fact that you are a professional in the field. The result is that you have been put in an uncomfortable position. You are getting paid for something that isn't benefiting the client, or you are forced to do something that goes against your professional judgment.

In some cases, this means that, whether you intend to or not, you are milking the account. Chances are, your tip-off here is a feeling of guilt or of time wasted.

"The biggest issue for us is that it's a distraction," says Gerald Westerbrook. "If we're not working together, moving forward on your plan as a client as with all our other clients, then we're just chasing our tails."

The principle of helping a client meet his or her goals far outweighs the collection of the retainer fee, Westerbrook says. "Seeing your client be successful is vital. It's a roadmap. It's a process. It's important to feel like you're doing your job for your client, and that your product is of value."

Sometimes a client is heading down a dangerous path and refuses your best advice. You are asked to go against your professional judgment.

"During the tech boom of the late 1990s, when dotcoms were going crazy, we had a few clients who wanted to get involved with those companies," says Westerbrook. "We wouldn't do it. As a result, these people left us. We would've had to drop them anyway when we had exhausted efforts to set them on the right path, but they were usually in such a hurry to "get rich" that they were willing to sever the relationship before we were. It was getting to the point where we were going to let them go anyway. It was in their worst interest to advise them in the way they wanted to be advised."

Westerbrook knew that investors in dotcoms were taking undue risks. A typical dotcom was a company whose defining characteristics included being an Internet presence instead of a brick-and-mortar location, with lots of venture capital raised, and an inflated stock price based on optimism and hype.

Sure enough, Westerbrook's instincts proved correct. The dotcom bubble burst. Paper fortunes deflated massively and quickly.

"With investing, there should always be some intrinsic value or fundamental reason for why you're going to invest in a company or other opportunity," Westerbrook says. "And if you can't justify an investment based on the basic tenets of investing, then you should never do it. If a client ignores your advice and wants you to proceed with a transaction, and you do, then you're just not good at what you do.

"It's like a lawyer saying, 'Go and do this,' when all the law books stacked on his shelf say, 'Don't do this.' There are certain guidelines a professional must follow. Any good businessman will tell you that you have to follow your guidelines and give your best professional service. If you don't, in the long run you're going to have unhappy clients."

Mark Goodman, the attorney in Reno, Nevada, has an active client base of all types of people. When it comes to dealing with certain toxic types he likes to refer to them as Shoppers, Nitpickers and Commodity Traders. Here are Mark's thoughts:

"The Shopper is the prospect who only seems to care about price. The Shopper bargains aggressively on price, rates and payment terms. Obviously, price is an important consideration when looking at any product or service, and I completely respect that. However, if the only thing you care about is price, I don't want to work with you. My staff routinely takes calls from people who (sometimes before even saying "hello") demand to know "How much do you charge for a trademark/contract/patent/whatever?" The Shopper will always wonder if they could have received a better price elsewhere.

"The Nitpicker is quite simply someone who over-aggressively nitpicks your work and/or your billing. Of course, I expect clients to review my work and provide input and to review my billing's accuracy. However, there are some people who pound you on every line item so hard that it's impossible to have an efficient business relationship. I literally had a client once dispute a 40 minute charge on a trademark office action stating that her uncle was a lawyer and that this trademark office action response should not have taken more than 20 minutes. I wonder why her uncle did not take this case?

"The Commodity Trader is someone that views you, your business and/or your staff to be a commodity—merely a resource at their disposal—rather than a human being engaged in critical thinking. The Commodity Trader does not seem to acknowledge or respect your needs and circumstances as a business owner or person. One client I think about in this regard is a guy who 1) demanded to be seen right away where there was no real urgency, 2) negotiated the retainer fairly aggressively, 3) demanded immediate appointments with no real urgency, 4) demanded the work be complete by arbitrary deadlines, 5) stiffed us on the back end of the bill even though he admitted that the work was satisfactory and the bill was reasonable. It was a modest bill, and I know he had enough money.

"Admittedly, the Toxic Commodity Trader can be harder to spot than most others, but it's worth keeping the concept in mind as it is so fundamental to your relationships with clients/customers. R "Ray" Wang wrote in the *Harvard Business Review* that business relationships flow on a spectrum from transactional to relationship-based. A transactional business relationship is where the provider and the client/customer do not have to interact very much, if at all. My relationship with the corner gas station is mostly transactional. I pop in my credit card, pump the gas and leave. The quality of gas seems uniform. My buying decision is based on convenience of location and price only. The gas station owner doesn't really care if I'm an obnoxious person, crazy or criminal. As long as I can operate the credit card machine and gas pump, we're good. Fortunately (or sometimes unfortunately), most businesses are relationship-based. Most businesses that you and I run involve a substantial, if not intimate, relationship between the provider and the client/customer. Managing these business relationships is a huge key to your business success.

"The Shopper, Nitpicker and Commodity Trader as potential clients share a common denominator. They view your business as a purely transactional one, like a gas station, when it's not. It is important to identify and avoid these types of clients."

Thank you, Mark.

A good working relationship with a client relies on you contributing your unique skills. Otherwise, you're simply an order-taker. And while appeasing clients and giving them what they want may be an easy way to earn a living in the short-term, in the long run it's a formula for disaster.

The client is usually too close to their problem to correctly diagnose the root causes. If you simply agree to help implement the client's preconceived solution you are not helping the client or your career. You won't be making a difference. Instead, you must bring your own expertise, objectivity and outside outlook to the table. You must help the client go back and address the real challenges, some of which they are too immersed in to identify. In this manner you become a strategic partner, to everyone's benefit.

Identifying the good clients, the ones you can help and succeed with, is a key to your business future. Identifying and dismissing the Toxic Clients is equally important. A friend of mine assigns a unique and shrill ring-tone for each Toxic Client. That is his strategy for identifying the problems that are a part of his business. The next step is to dismiss...

Chapter Eleven:

Dismiss

"Those disputing, contradicting and confuting people are generally unfortunate in their affairs. They get victory sometimes, but they never get good will, which would be of more use to them."
~ Benjamin Franklin

Toxic Clients are frequently misunderstood. First and foremost is the mistaken idea that they are cognizant of their own behavior. They usually are not. While the terms "self-righteous" and "self-interested" certainly apply to toxic personalities, ironically the term "self-reflective" usually does not.

Most Toxic Clients have a huge blind spot equal to a reflecting mirror on how they behave. They can't 'see' how they are acting and are thus shocked by any criticism of their actions. Attempting to spell out and set right their behavior is not a productive use of your time. You can't change what they don't (or won't) recognize.

Expecting to reason with a Toxic Client in the hopes of altering their behavior and saving the relationship is futile. As psychologist Dr. Kenji Sax advises: "The only thing you can do is adjust your behavior."

If you find yourself with a Toxic Client on your hands, you have a choice to make: Will you accept the behavior or fire the client? You may feel the relationship is worth saving, and that's your prerogative. However, it may actually be a more profitable decision for you to fire the client.

Sandy Roth's advertising agency has now arrived at this point. She has seen that pruning clientele can ultimately create more profits. She likens this process to the farmers who grow giant, prize winning vegetables at the county fair. By removing the less promising vegetables from the vine the promising ones succeed. And so do you.

Don't forget the Pareto Principle. The least profitable segment of your clientele takes four times as much of your time as the most profitable. Your job is to shift that proportion so that you can nurture the clients who bring you fulfillment and income.

Gerald Westerbrook feels that keeping bad clients says as much about his reputation as it does theirs. "When your values are compromised by any one client you lose those values. Either you stray off course or you let the client go and stay true to your North Star. For our business there is no in-between. Our reputation, through our values, is more important than any one client."

But once you make up your mind to fire a Toxic Client, how do you go about it? Few of us enjoy conflict, and even fewer of us relish creating situations in which our professional reputations are jeopardized. This fear of angering a client may keep us paralyzed.

Unfortunately, the only actions you can control are your own. Whether a client gets on social media and badmouths you or spreads a rumor around town that you're unprofessional, all you can do is ensure that you've behaved as responsibly as possible. Know that you have dotted your i's and crossed your t's so that the client won't come back to haunt you. Be sure that you operate through a corporation or LLC so that your personal assets are not exposed to a litigious Toxic Client. If you conduct business in your individual name with a sole proprietorship, both your company and personal assets can be reached in a lawsuit. Toxic Clients can be vindictive and will prey upon such a weakness in your business structure. Always operate through a protected entity.

What are your options for dismissing a Toxic Client? Should you do such a bad job that the client fires you first? Perhaps in an extreme situation this might work, but chances are your professional pride will interfere. If you're like most business owners, you always try your best, and derive your satisfaction from a job well done. Performing poorly may make you feel worse about the situation.

Should you play dead and avoid the client's calls and messages in the hopes that they go away? In Case No. 16: The HVAC owner, Karl Richards determined that avoidance was the only way to deal with tar baby Jimmy Zolezzi. While Karl preferred to be forthcoming in most of his dealings he saw forbearance as his only way out. Your own solutions will vary according to each specific situation. But avoiding a client is clearly not the right call in every case.

Lesson #11: You can't reason with or fix a Toxic Client. The only actions you can control are your own, which may mean firing the client.

While there may be (as sung by Paul Simon) 50 Ways To Leave Your Lover, there really are only six good methods for relieving yourself of a Toxic Client:

1. Prioritize your 20 percent.
2. Devise a schedule or policy that no longer accommodates the Toxic Clients.
3. Send the client to the competition like a bad penny.
4. Raise your rates.
5. Charge a "Pain in the Ass" (PITA) fee.
6. Fire the client outright.

1. Prioritize your 20 percent.

As discussed, your job is to nurture the 20 percent of your clientele that are the stars, the good clients. Sandy Roth suggests this strategy for putting your money where your mouth is. "When the good clients call, they get serviced first. The cringe-worthy clients get pushed to the back of the line." She adds that eventually the cringe-inducing clients will take the hint.

Clients forced to take a backseat may either come to understand that you're simply not going to drop everything for their unreasonable or last-minute requests, or they'll take their business elsewhere.

When it comes to paying Sandy says, "Fast pays get fast work." When people call for more work to be done who owe money from previous jobs Sandy says, "Never avoid the discussion of payment. If you aren't paying I'm not working." Such a policy prioritizes the good clients over the bad.

2. Devise a schedule that no longer accommodates the client.

This is a great method for avoiding conflict. It's a great "It's not you, it's me" trick that likely won't rub the client the wrong way. Yes, like with dating it may be dishonest, but it's a white lie. As mentioned, the custom in Germany is that if you tell a white lie to save your business, it's not considered a harmful lie. And so it is in this case: It doesn't hurt anyone. And it saves you having to outright fire the client (which may be a lot more painful), so it could be your safest bet for dismissing a Toxic Client.

There are a few ways to do this. One way is to tell the client that you're (conveniently) restructuring your business to eliminate the services he or she wants, or to focus on a particular niche area. For instance, if you have a marketing firm, you can tell your Toxic Client in the hotel business that you've decided to focus on marketing for the health care industry, and will be referring out any non-health-care-related business.

Another method is to defer to an imaginary non-compete clause.

Tell the Toxic Client that you've recently been reminded of, or just entered into, a contract with another major client in the same industry. Tell the client that the clause specifically states that you may not do work for his or her competitors, so you'll have to part ways immediately. If you actually select one of your other clients to pin this on, you may want to give them a heads up and get their okay first. Of course, this is to the good client's benefit so hopefully they will understand and accept.

Or, you can just say you're too busy. This is a simple way to avoid doing business with a Toxic Client, and it's often not being dishonest to say so. You could say something to the effect of, "I'm sorry, we're booked up for the next three months," "Our next available opening won't be until next year," "We're short-staffed at the moment and I don't know when we'll be able to accommodate you," or simply "We're not taking on any new business at the moment."

This method may not be 100 percent foolproof. Remember, Toxic Clients usually don't realize they're toxic, and may never get the hint that you're avoiding them. And if they're like Shirley, the mentally ill customer at Jenna Starr's salon (Case No. 12: The Beauty Salon), they may have already been shunned from every other business in town and have no other option but to continue calling you. All you can do is remain firm until the client goes away.

3. Send the client to the competition like a bad penny.

The phrase "A bad penny always turns up" means that people you find unpleasant have a way of reappearing in your life. In business, this means that a toxic customer is likely to keep returning to you. Often your best strategy is to pass this cursed coin onto your competitors.

Sometimes you will do this on the initial contact with a customer. As Case No. 3: The Dermatologist illustrated, every couple of months, one difficult individual or another will phone or show up at Dr. Sarah Adam's busy dermatology practice insisting to be seen right away, although the waiting list is usually set four to eight weeks out. Her staff has a policy for dealing with such pushy people. "We'll say, 'Oh, we can't accommodate you. You'll have to go down the street.' We'll give them some names of other practitioners. And then we don't have to worry about them."

Financial advisor Gerald Westerbrook uses this diplomatic method when firing a client who refuses to follow his firm's counsel: "We're graduating you."

Westerbrook cites the example of a client who was a pleasant man, a widower in his early sixties whose children were grown. The man owned a nice home, and his mortgage was paid off. He had just retired from a professional career in which he'd earned an annual salary in the high six figures and he had saved several million towards retirement. He wanted to enjoy a comfortable retirement, so he hired Westerbrook to come up with a financial plan in the hope that the investment income would help him to sustain his good lifestyle for at least 20 years.

With more than 15 years of experience in the financial field as an analyst, portfolio manager, and strategist, Westerbrook works on a retainer basis, typically with clients whose net worth ranges from $2 million to $30 million.

After reviewing the man's financial situation, Westerbrook determined that he was a good fit for the firm's services and decided to take him on as a client. Westerbrook came up with a plan that covered all the bases: the man's current assets; his spending budget; a rate of return that would yield sufficient spending money for the retirement lifestyle he desired; the number of years the man expected to live outside of an assisted-living facility; and the necessary insurance to meet this older gentleman's present and future needs.

Westerbrook allocated the man's capital into a diversified mix of assets: stocks, bonds, real estate, private equity, and energy assets. Each year, the portfolio would be adjusted according to performances and patterns in the different markets, and to balance the mix of income and growth investments. The final plan called for an 8 percent annual return to maintain the man's desired lifestyle.

At the beginning, the returns were averaging 12 percent. All would have been fine were it not for one shortcoming: the man's spending habits. During his first year as Westerbrook's client, the man consistently exceeded his stated budget. He was unwilling or unable to stick to the financial plan. He was always buying a gift for a friend, tuition for a niece, a trip to the Canadian Rockies, or an expensive suit. Although there were few big-ticket items, these smaller expenditures, collectively, usually took him over budget.

As a result, Westerbrook's client was eroding his asset base.

Instead of benefiting from compounding interest, he was dipping into his annual gains. And what's more is that the man couldn't accept the fact that his extra purchases were adding up.

Westerbrook met with the man once every four months to review his portfolio. Westerbrook pointed out to the client that he was spending more than he was supposed to from his gains and even taking money from his principle. Westerbrook explained to him that the 12 percent earnings—four points higher than projected—would take care of the extra spending for a while, but that the extra gains wouldn't always be there.

The older gentleman seemed to be in denial. He always had excuses for his impulsive expenditures: "My car broke down," or, "It snowed so much in Utah last week, I just had to go skiing." Sometimes he'd simply argue, "Look, I have to live my life!"

Westerbrook tried to reason with him. "He usually left with some acknowledgment that he had to curtail the extra spending and adhere to the program," Westerbrook says. "But there was never a complete buy-in.

"And six months later, he'd end up right back in the same situation." This pattern went on for nearly four years.

Finally, enough was enough. It became apparent that the man was not willing to commit to the plan he'd hired Westerbrook to devise, and the relationship clearly was not going to work. He made the tough decision, after four years, to fire the client.

"He didn't accept the fact that he needed to change his life," Westerbrook recalls. "He thought he could go along living the same way as when his wife was alive and earning income, too. He wasn't realistic—or maybe he wanted us to perform magic."

At their next meeting, Westerbrook announced to the man that he would be "graduating."

"Our services are no longer a fit for you," Westerbrook told him. He handed the man a list of other financial advisors whom Westerbrook respected, and explained that the transfer of the account would be handled efficiently.

The man was completely surprised by the news, but it ended up being the best thing for him. While he didn't curtail his spending habits, the man ended up taking a part-time job to offset the spending—a recommendation Westerbrook had made in year one. Westerbrook notes that the shock of being fired sometimes brings a Toxic Client back to earth, which can be a positive development.

Westerbrook adds the caveat that the professional thing to do is to give a head's up to a competitor about the client's toxicity. After all, what goes around comes around. At some point, it may be your turn to have a bad penny rolled your way. You'd want to be warned.

Here's something else to consider: A referral doesn't necessarily have to be a bad thing. While some will not take on such a client others will appreciate the challenge. Ultimately, you might find that someone else is a better fit for the client, and the relationship is good for all concerned. If you can make such an arrangement, you've done a good thing. It's a good idea to follow up with a referral to ensure that you haven't left the client feeling ditched, and that you're doing what you can to preserve your reputation.

4. Raise your rates.

"If you really want to see bad clients head the other way, raise your prices," says house painter Scott McGee "Not just by 10 or 15 percent. Raise them so they are prohibitively high. In the very rare case someone accepts you'll be paid very well for dealing with their toxicity."

Landscape contractor Marvin Washington has tried this tactic. "If I suspect a client may prove to be difficult, I deliberately give an excessively high bid. Most people wouldn't accept it, and if the person does, it might be worth the trouble."

5. Charge a "Pain in the Ass" (PITA) fee.

Similar to the rate hike, the PITA fee is a charge you apply to Toxic Clients' bills just because they were a pain in the ass to deal with—taking forever to approve estimates or finished work, nickel-and-diming you about every item on the bill, being disorganized, changing their minds, being rude, or making unreasonable demands as the narcissist did with Eric the car salesman.

You can tack on this charge in a couple of ways: You can tack on an additional percentage (say, 20 percent) to the overall bill as an administrative fee. Any contract you have should allow for this charge. You can show the charge on the bill as time spent on labor. If the client sees that all those last-minute phone calls to change orders are being billed, they might be less inclined to take up your time in the future. Some businesses (for instance, graphic designers) may even charge "rush fees," which are fees tacked onto a bill for having dropped what they were doing to accommodate a client's last-minute request.

Remember that if the client opts not to pay the fee, you can send that bad penny elsewhere.

6. Fire the client outright.

This is the last resort for dealing with a Toxic Client. It's one of the most unpleasant tasks in business, but is vital to your business' well-being (and, sometimes, your own personal well-being).

Firing a client means communicating clearly and decisively that the business relationship is terminated. It need not be done with hostility; in fact, professionalism dictates that a confrontational manner should be avoided as much as possible. But the firing must be done with absolute clarity and finality.

There are times when doing this verbally is sufficient—for example, a hair-salon owner telling a customer that his or her patronage is no longer welcome. The hair stylists and skin and nail professionals in Jenna Starr's salon are independent contractors. If a customer complains about a job, the stylist will try to make it right, putting in extra time. But on rare occasions, a customer won't give the stylist a chance to make it right, and instead will demand their money back. The stylist typically will refund the payment minus the cost of hair products used. The stylist will also make clear that the customer's business is no longer welcome at the establishment, saying something like, "We just feel that we can't please you here, and you will probably be better served elsewhere." It's diplomatic, but firm.

There are times when ending the relationship should and must be done in writing. If you have a contract requiring a written notice of termination, follow the terms of the contract. If the situation appears problematic, or confusing given the contractual provisions, consult with an attorney.

If a Toxic Client refuses to leave the premises when asked to, it becomes a legal matter: Trespassing. You may have to call the police. You may file a police report and follow up with a letter stating that the person is not to return.

Regardless of how you do it, there are certain circumstances in which you absolutely should, without hesitation or guilt, fire a client outright:

- The client is abusive.
- The client doesn't pay.

An abusive client absolutely must be axed. After client George Stinson (Case No. 5: The Financial Planner) verbally attacked Gerald Westerbrook over the phone for what Stinson mistakenly perceived as a poor performance on his variable annuities account, Westerbrook hung up on him. Then he faxed Stinson a letter saying that he was resigning the account, and directing Stinson to transfer his funds elsewhere.

Once a client becomes abusive, there is no other course but to fire him or her, Westerbrook says, because if the client is retained, he or she will simply become an energy drain. "From that point forward, all they'll do is battle me. I'll give them a recommendation, and they'll second-guess me. It's a waste of time and energy. They beat up your staff, they're continually upset, and they're a cancerous virus that impedes everybody."

In his book *Get off the Couch! Seven Psychological Secrets for Success in Business,* author Kenji Sax writes that some people are "fishing for you to lose control and show inappropriate behavior so that they can say to themselves and others that you were the one who was in the wrong. It's hard to believe that some people want you to lose control, but there are those that are so angry at the world that they want the world to be angry back."

When Sax understands that he's in a situation where he can't reason with a customer who is acting inappropriately, he employs a tactic that he calls "a mirror, reflecting back what you see in their behavior." It's a change in argument style, and it's conducted in an unruffled manner.

"If somebody's yelling and screaming, I'll say, 'What I'm noticing is you're really upset, because you're yelling at me, and I'm trying to help you resolve this situation. You're making it very, very difficult for me. I need you to calm down."

It is critical in such interactions never to lose control of your own emotions, and never to raise your voice when interacting with an abusive client, no matter how much you want to grab the person by the collar and toss them out the door.

"Negative emotion doesn't belong in business, particularly when you're dealing with customers," Sax says. "You want to set an example for your employees, and also maintain the dignity of your practice, the high standards."

Clients with substance-abuse problems are abusive in their own way. They often conceal their vices during initial contacts. Landscape contractor Marvin Washington will never forget the time he installed a sprinkler system and hydro-seeded 10,000 square feet of lawn for a client—a retired trucking-company owner. The job went well, the client was cordial, and the bill was paid in a timely fashion. So it was quite a surprise when the client filed a complaint with the state contractors' board after his water bill went sky high.

"He was sure we'd done something wrong when installing the irrigation system, even though there was no evidence of leakage anywhere," recalls Washington. "The real problem was that he'd fallen off the wagon and he was a nasty drunk."

Both Washington and a representative from the contractors' board tried to appease the client, who was uncooperative. When Washington went to his door one afternoon to talk with him, the client greeted him with a highball in hand and nasty words spilling from his mouth. The contractors' board rep finally got so fed up with the abusive behavior of the man that he put an end to all dealings with him.

Interestingly, Washington ran into the man a few years later, and he behaved rather normally, as if he had no recollection of the events. "He was off the sauce, apparently, and totally reasonable again!" says Washington.

Of course, the easiest client to fire is the one who doesn't pay you. In such a situation, you lose nothing by cutting the client loose, and he or she hasn't a leg to stand on in terms of retaining your services. If you've done things the right way, you have a contract spelling out the terms of engagement. As long as you've provided what you've agreed to provide, feel free to pursue collection if you haven't been paid.

Some customers will go so far as to throw a tirade just to get out of paying. They want to embarrass you in front of all your customers. They want to goad and pressure you to accept a significant discount in fees. They want to shame you into granting their toxic wish. As was illustrated in the chapter on Freeloaders, restaurant managers see these people all the time. They are the patrons who complain that the meat was undercooked, there was a hair in the food, or there was some other shortcoming or health hazard. The common policy is to waive their bills. But, as we discussed, free can create problems. Free can attract more freeloaders. Consider replacing the meal, but still get paid for it.

Jenna Starr occasionally sees variations of this scam in her salon. She describes one woman who told her manicurist not to cut her cuticles because she didn't like them cut. The manicurist pushed the cuticles back and continued the manicure. Afterward, the client refused to pay because her cuticles were still there.

"If we refund on anything, we make it clear that the customer doesn't need to come back," Jenna says.

Human behavior runs on a spectrum, and there are, unfortunately, a small number of people who try to get something for nothing. They are deadbeats. They don't intend to pay for goods or services rendered.

Sometimes they don't have the means to pay. Other times they have much more than the means to pay, but they do not have good character. They aren't worth having as customers, or as sources for referrals. They are deadbeats and must be fired.

A woman had a laser-hair removal procedure at the dermatology office Kenny Adams managed. Her $400 check bounced. Adams called her up to tell her payment was due. She responded that the procedure had not worked, and she did not intend to pay.

"Come on in and at least let us look at it," Adams offered. "Let us evaluate you. We may just do it over again for you, at no extra charge."

"No," she replied stridently. "I'm NOT coming in."

That was a clear sign to Adams that he was dealing with a scam artist. It was time to sever the relationship. He referred her account to a collection agency, where an agent informed him that this wasn't the first time the woman had pulled such a stunt. She apparently had a pattern of bouncing checks to dermatology businesses.

In many counties across the country the local District Attorney will go after individuals who write and bounce checks. You may want to see if they can help you with a toxic check writer.

Keeping the Devil You Know

Every rule has its exception. There are times when keeping a Toxic Client is the best strategy. The most obvious example is when the client represents a reliable and substantial source of income, such as a long-term client with a proven track record of paying on time and providing repeat business. In Case No. 4: The Sales Person, Ellen Bay determined that client John Minden's anger was justified. He was not toxic but rather a good client worth keeping. It was appropriate to rescue and rebuild the relationship.

Chapter Twelve:

Avoid

"If you don't know where you're going,
you'll end up somewhere else."
~ Yogi Berra

By now, you can see that it is almost inevitable that a Toxic Client will come knocking at your door at some point in your career.

Remember the sampling of business owners mentioned at the start:

95% have encountered Toxic Clients

80% have dealt with non-paying clients

50% have been stiffed (never paid)

40% regularly deal with clients who take longer than 90 days to pay.

As we've said before, the customer is not always right.

Knowing that you will encounter a Toxic Client is the first step to avoiding them. The next step is to set up a security system that enables you to detect the danger in advance. The third and final step is knowing how to minimize the damage if the problem individual does, indeed, get in your door.

The security system I refer to has four basic components:

- Conducting research on the client
- Noting potential red flags for toxicity

- Setting up retainers and other advance payments
- Protecting yourself with clear contracts.

Conduct Research on All Potential Clients

One of my clients, a consultant, researches every customer before accepting an assignment. She checks the client's website and other Google postings. She searches the Internet for other consultant's comments. She checks with the Better Business Bureau for complaints, many of which can be quite revealing. While she takes some complaints with a grain of salt, she has come to instinctively know which ones seem real.

These are great methods for conducting preliminary research, but for long-term engagements with clients, it's a good idea to conduct a screening interview.

An initial screening interview is a standard practice with many businesses—even if it's only asking the customer what goods or services he or she is looking for. In an elementary way, the counter people at sandwich shops and hair salons do this: "What can I get you?" or "What are you in for today?" If a customer isn't in the sandwich shop for a sub or a side order of chips or a brownie, but instead wants a burger, the business is of course turned away or referred elsewhere. If a customer goes into a chain salon looking for a perm or other expensive styling service, the customer may be told that this isn't the sort of service the salon offers, and that another salon with boutique services will be the appropriate choice.

A screening interview will determine very quickly if your business is right for the client, and vice versa. The screening interview can help filter out Toxic Clients before you take them on.

The interview can be rather informal, and even conducted over the telephone with a simple "How did you hear about us?"

Referrals from friends or acquaintances are often desirable because like-minded people usually associate with each other. If your professional and social circles are characterized by positive, energetic doers, then a referral from someone in these groups will likely yield a decent client.

Note, however, that this is not a screening method that can be relied upon 100 percent—even your friends can be Toxic Clients to other people. A more reliable method of gathering information about a prospective client might be to run a credit check. If this is an option for your business, it can be an excellent way to weed out clients who have trouble paying.

Further Due Diligence

Frank Troppe suggests the following methods for avoiding Toxic Clients:

- Seek out the healthy relationships you want rather than passively waiting for inquires. If you are intentional about the kind of clients you want, you will take a more active versus passive role in shaping your future.

- Conduct due diligence on potential clients before accepting them.

- Be honest with yourself, and don't take on new clients out of desperation.

- Remember your instincts, and use them to avoid clients that give you a bad feeling.

- Discuss and outline all project details before reaching an agreement.

Troppe also suggests the following strategy: Spend just a little more time this week with the clients you enjoy most. Talk about their business or interests – see if there is a part of their network you can also serve and begin swapping out low-reward interactions for those that feel better. Can you imagine if you could have replaced the worst 15 minutes of last week with the best 15 minutes of this week? My best clients help me do that, and that's what I do for them as well.

As Troppe and other entrepreneurs point out, there are various red flags to watch for in the screening interview and throughout the initial process of onboarding a new client. The earliest red flag may be the client's insistence to be served right away, even if an appointment hasn't been scheduled. Consider the pushy woman on the phone in Case No. 3: The Dermalogist, who demanded to be seen immediately in Kenny Adams' clinic. When told that would be impossible, she started spewing insults.

Accommodating patrons who want their appointments immediately is one of the trickiest parts of hair-salon owner Jenna Starr's business.

Customers with gift certificates sometimes act as if they deserve to get in right away—even though a slip of paper accompanying each certificate advises that appointments may need to be scheduled four to six weeks in advance. The only other option is having a name put on a cancellation list in case a spot opens.

One woman whose gift certificate was a birthday present from her husband thought that the certificate entitled her to special privileges in setting an appointment. It didn't. Frustrated, she asked that her husband get his money back. Jenna was happy to accommodate the request.

"It was a client we didn't want to deal with," Jenna said. "When they're difficult before you ever have to work with them, it's better not to *ever* have to work with them."

The same goes for all businesses. Better that these problem individuals are screened out before their business is taken.

Take Note of the Red Flags

As you've been reading this book, I hope you've begun spotting the red flags of toxicity on your own. Sometimes it's easier to see them when you are an outside observer, looking in.

The red flags come in many forms. Sometimes they're in the form of off-handed comments casually tossed out in conversation by the prospective client. Sometimes a person's bad reputation precedes them.

Sometimes you get a bad feeling in your gut. Remember, research tells us that our gut instincts are usually correct—don't ignore it!

Here are some standard red flags for toxicity that you should be on the lookout for:

- Negative comments
- A bad reputation
- Over-eagerness
- Asking for the impossible
- Questionable terms and conditions
- Your internal alarm goes off

Negative comments

As an experienced accountant, Victor Lee (Case No. 2: The CPA) knows that tax season is a stressful time for anyone. For someone with IRS troubles, that stress is further compounded. Clients may deal with this stress in a number ways: Some are always nervous, while others grow testy. This doesn't necessarily mean that all clients exhibiting these signs are toxic. Other red flags might suggest that. One of these is a tendency to make negative or disparaging comments.

When John Yang entered Victor Lee's office and began complaining about his previous accountant, he was actually waving a red flag in front of Lee's face. In retrospect, Lee knows that he should have listened more actively and carefully. Anybody who disparages an entire profession probably has a negative outlook on life, and will be difficult to deal with. Rather than dealing with his own shortcomings or failings, he blames others. And these kinds of people don't make for good clients.

If a client makes outrageous, blanket negative comments, or statements that indicate irrational hostility, it's a sign the client may be too toxic to work with.

A bad reputation

Personal trainer Matthew Martinez takes a client's poor reputation with others as a serious warning sign. In retrospect, he would have passed on working with wealthy businessman Jeff Kerry (Case No. 1: The Personal Trainer) after another of Martinez's clients had mentioned that Kerry was known to shortchange construction contractors on engineering projects.

After getting burned by Kerry, Martinez now understands that what a person is worth in the financial department doesn't equate to what he or she is worth in the character department. A rich person can be as tight, or tighter, than one of modest means. In this case, Martinez would have held back the precious time slots he gave to Kerry and waited for a new prospect to show up. Martinez would have given Kerry an excuse about lacking any openings, and turned him away.

"Looking back, I would have listened to the people who told me not to train him because he doesn't pay his bills."

We all like to think, "That won't happen to me." We have a hard time believing that we would fall for the tricks others have fallen for. But the fact is, we often do. As business people, we are optimists and want to believe the best in people. But the next time you hear bad information about a client, don't dismiss it. Instead, either address it with the client or put systems into place that ward off such behavior.

Over-eagerness

Remember that a good client is one who screens you, too.

A warning sign for marketing agency owner Sandy Roth was how quickly her firm was brought in by St. Anselm's Healthcare to replace the agency that it was considering firing (Case No. 11: The Marketing Firm). The entire transaction happened within 24 hours.

"They didn't do due diligence on us," Roth says. "They hired us basically from meeting with us once; they didn't ask for references or talk with other people we worked with. They did it based on personality. When you're spending that kind of money, it's not a good business decision."

In other words, if it seems too good to be true, it probably is.

Asking for the impossible

There are only 24 hours in a day. There is only so much work your business can handle. There are limits to the outcomes you can guarantee. Jenna Starr cannot promise that you will look like a celebrity after she gives you a haircut. Some clients, however, are looking for miracles. Miracles are not your business. If a client cannot accept this, the client should be politely turned away.

Another impossible demand is one that would force you to violate your best professional judgment. When Gerald Westerbrook refused to invest clients' assets in over-hyped dotcoms and they balked, he was content to see these clients take their business elsewhere.

In this vein, there are some services Jenna Starr discourages the hairstylists in her salon from performing. "If somebody's hair is in really bad shape," Jenna says, "I may say, 'Your hair is already bleached so much we can't perm it because it could fall out.' Sometimes a client will offer to sign a waiver accepting the risk, but we'll still refuse. We don't want that person walking around as an advertisement for us."

The principle that Starr and Westerbrook operate on is that every job for a client translates into advertising for the business. When a client's needs have been well taken care of it speaks volumes as to the skill and integrity of the business. In Jenna's salon, for example, the work performed by the stylists—even though they are independent contractors—reflects on the entire salon. If customers' hair, nails, and skin look terrific, these results drive more business to the salon. On the other hand, a job that doesn't deliver results, even if it was in the course of trying to carry out a client's impossible wishes, equals negative advertising.

They call things 'impossible' for a good reason. The impossible is not possible. Stick with clients who accept the possible.

Questionable financial terms

The client may propose an out-of-the-ordinary payment process that would be considered "non-standard." For example, the client may suggest bartering for services, or paying only when the job is complete. Or the client may insist on paying what he or she believes your product or services are worth, not what you say the price is.

All of these things are red flags.

A Word About Doing Business Internationally

The clients whose stories are told in the pages of this book can be universally understood by any American business owner. But it's a big world, full of other countries and people who do business differently, and who interact differently with others. Many of the rules we've discussed here can't be strictly applied to clients beyond our borders. There are times when clients' instructions may be unclear, or when their mannerisms or ways of speaking immediately strike you as uncomfortable because they are unfamiliar, but they may not necessarily be toxic.

In my book *Writing Winning Business Plans*, I wrote that a common mistake business owners make is that they treat the "international market" as if it's one place. There are many of nations in the world, each of them with its own language, customs, history and economy. Applying U.S. (or your home country's) standards to every other nation can be a huge error.

Chief among such mistakes is not understanding how contracts work overseas. While a contract is an essential document for protecting your rights as a business owner here in the U.S., a contract may not mean the same thing overseas. In some countries contracts are viewed as suggestions or outlines for how to proceed. They may carry nowhere near the force of the law that they do in America.

It's crucial that you thoroughly research and understand the laws, people, economy, and customs of any country with which you're considering doing business. You must know the laws to ensure you don't break them. You must know how marketing works in that country if you want to sell your products there. And you must know how to avoid offending others if you're going to work with people from other countries.

Try to understand how foreign clients behave in business meetings or one-on-one conversations. The gesture or terminology that might immediately offend you could be commonplace in another land.

In some countries, it isn't customary for women to engage in business dealings. An American woman might perceive this in a first interaction with a foreign client and immediately rule the client out as toxic. But this person may simply be behaving in the accustomed manner he would at home. You certainly have the choice to not deal with such a person or culture. But if you do move forward, will you be making things less toxic for future generations? I don't have the answer.

Similarly, many cultures value the group over the individual, meaning that it would be rude for you to presume that one person can quickly approve a job or make a unilateral decision. Such situations may require a bit more clarity in communication, and some time to adapt to, but this doesn't necessarily mean the client is toxic. (Know that your direct American style may be considered toxic by them!) You may want to suspend judgment until you learn the lay of their land. But screen all clients thoroughly. As with all situations, dismiss the clients who exhibit toxicity.

Whether domestically or internationally, sometimes the big, bright dollar signs from a new prospect can blind you to a client's toxicity.

Remember Case No. 11: The Marketing Firm. Sandy Roth says, "In business, you get caught up in the prospect of a big account or big money, and you 'Pollyanna' over the other things." Roth was so elated about landing the contract with the large health care chain that she missed some important warning signs.

There were two initial red flags signaling that the health care company account had chronic problems and wasn't solid enough to build a new agency around—which Roth tried to do, recruiting three partners, leasing a larger office space and hiring staff.

The first red flag was the client's board of directors' 6-5 vote giving Roth's agency the account. One of the directors, a long-timer with the company, was upset that the incumbent agency hadn't been retained. That meant a critical opponent could be working against the advertising/marketing campaign that Roth's and her partners were to create and implement. And this turned out to be true. (To make matters worse, the upset director was soon after promoted to chief operating officer—the third most powerful executive.)

The second red flag of impending distress was that the client's board members decided, not long after inking the contract with Roth's agency, that they'd overestimated their company's situation, and they reduced the maximum budget for yearly ad expenditures from $5 million to $3 million. "It was a sign they didn't have a good idea of what they were going to spend," says Roth, "or where they were going to spend it."

She likens such business situations to the dating scene, when romance appears to blossom. You may be addled by attraction at the start and only gain clarity later. "In a bad relationship," Roth says, "you look back and the signs are there right from the beginning."

It would have been better to withhold a full business and leasehold commitment instead of planning a future around the other party.

Roth learned the same lesson from her experience with the next big healthcare account that came her agency's way. In fact, it followed so closely on the heels of the terminated relationship with Prompt and Caring that it could be considered a "rebound."

In retrospect, Roth should have been wary of being hired by a company that had just fired its local ad agency and needed to hire a new one ASAP. The printouts of email exchanges she was shown between the fired agency and the client should have triggered concern, she says.

"When you date somebody, you need to see how he treated his ex- wife—someone he used to love and no longer does," says Roth. "The client left the other agency owing it money. There had been a lot of petty squabbling. We should have seen it coming."

Be on the lookout for any client who dismisses the use of a contract. They bemoan the old days when your word was your bond and a handshake sealed a deal. Beware of such patter. If they want to do a handshake deal say that once the contract is signed you'll be happy to shake hands.

Also beware of the incessant low baller. It is fine for a client to ask if this is your lowest price. That is normal. But when the same question is asked over and over and over again consider ending your agony. Tell the client to look elsewhere.

Lesson #12: The best way to overcome the challenge of a Toxic Client is to avoid working with one in the first place.

Your internal alarm sounds

If it doesn't feel right, there's a reason. Our instincts operate on a subconscious level, and recognize signs that our conscious minds may dismiss. Don't ignore the wisdom of your instincts.

Landscape contractor Marvin Washington wished he'd listened to his inner voice when something he couldn't put his finger on made him wary of the Collingsworths.

Washington says, "I realize I hadn't liked these people from the beginning, but I couldn't have said why. When your sixth sense tries to tell you something, you probably should listen."

Bottom line: If your instincts say run, run.

Clear Contracts

As you get into business you will want to have the proper contracts in place governing the terns of your service, any warranties and all payment terms. Please beware of the internet forms that 'look good enough'. They may be completely inappropriate for your specific situation. The assistance of an attorney is always suggested for the drafting of documents key to your business. You may not need the attorney for every contract. If they can provide you with a good template you should be fine for most transactions.

In some cases your client will provide you with one of their contracts. Please read it carefully. If the terms seem unclear or unfair to you don't gloss over your concern. You may be right on the money (and by signing it losing money).

There can be several sources of uncertainty in contract language. One is ambiguity. If an agreement states, "The artist shall paint the model nude," then who shows up without clothing? The model or the artist? You want to avoid contracts that can be interpreted in more than one way.

Vagueness is another source of contractual uncertainty. If you agree to perform services in a reasonable amount of time you may intend that to mean within 30 days. But that same time frame could mean 30 minutes to a dying client.

Strive for clarity in all your contracts. Put away the Latin dictionary. Use plain language at all times. If your client's contract is not clear to you question it and change it to meet your understanding.

Know that Toxic Clients will use an unclear contract as a feegoading strategy. They will mention that for each side to pay their attorneys to interpret a contested term will cost everyone. They will argue it is more prudent for you to accept a discounted amount to resolve the matter. A clear contract will minimize the pressure for abatement.

Setting up retainers and other advance payments

Personal trainer Matthew Martinez hasn't been burned by a non-paying client since his unhappy experience with wealthy businessman Jeff Kerry. That client had simply not showed up for four sessions in a row, having left the country on a trip without first informing Martinez, who was left waiting during precious hours he could have filled with paying clients.

Martinez told the health club where he worked to bill the client anyway. The client's wife had called up and insisted the charge be removed. Martinez, who already had given the club notice that he was resigning to start his own business and didn't want to leave any ill will behind, finally agreed to reimburse the client's account out of his own pocket.

Since going into business for himself, Martinez handles matters very differently. "At the club," he says, "I had a boss. And I was leaving at the time, and didn't want to make any waves. It's a small town. I wanted to leave a clean slate, with everybody happy when I left. Now it would be a little different. If I make the rules, and I break them, it's my own problem."

Martinez's rules as a self-employed personal trainer are very clear to all who hire him. All clients sign waivers saying they work out at their own risk. Those recovering from surgeries or accidents, or whose heart rates are out of whack for their ages, must obtain releases from their physicians.

And everyone pays in advance.

"They buy packages of 12 or 24 sessions. If they re-up, they buy a new package. But they pay before we play."

Martinez's business is thriving. He's busy eight to ten hours a day.

He has a strong client base, built on client referrals. He has a variety of clients, both young and old, including athletes. But most of his clientele are housewives ages 40 to 50 who like to keep their figures toned.

Word of mouth is his best advertising. It's a built-in screening process. People with similar lifestyles and similar spending habits often hang out together and share information. If a client can afford to pay, usually the friend the client refers also can afford to pay. If a prospect calls Martinez sight unseen, the caller is invited to visit Martinez's website to learn about his services and prices.

"It's usually the prices that turn people off," he says. "It's not inexpensive. That's usually the qualifier right there."

Regular clients sometimes try to avoid paying up front, but Martinez has cut this annoyance down to a minimum, thanks to the advance-payment packages. "I have some people, when their last session has run out, crying, 'My payment's coming,' or, 'I can pay you next week,' and want to schedule their next workout.

"I'll say, 'Well, let's wait until next week, then we can start again. Call me when you're ready to pay.'"

It's also a good idea to maintain a payment history for each client. This assists you in establishing measures that get you paid. Someone who has paid late more than once, for example, might be converted to a pay-in-advance schedule for all future jobs.

Enforcing Clear Contracts

A contract provides strong legal protection. But it doesn't all by itself guarantee that a Toxic Client won't try to violate your business agreement. Sometimes you must enforce a contract. And that involves hiring a good lawyer.

In the case of a truly Toxic Client, such as the Collingsworths, a written contract won't be enough to force the client to honor your legal rights.

Landscape contractor Marvin Washington had provided a written estimate to the Collingsworths. After the work was done, they refused to pay.

Washington would now file a mechanics' lien, which he calls "a powerful tool that will get anyone's attention." Washington also offers this piece of advice: "It helps to have a relationship with a good lawyer before you need one."

Fortunately, he happened to have one. "When you're in business," Washington says, "you can't allow yourself the luxury of being timid. We went to court three times, and I prevailed."

It is your choice to enforce a contract or not. For many business owners, the enforcement of payment maybe handled by an independent collection agency. More information on these agencies is found in Appendix C.

Consent forms can provide another layer of protection. Some consent forms are required by law. The treatments clients receive at the dermatology office managed by Kenny Adams are not foolproof. No cosmetic treatments are. Wrinkles might not fully disappear. Hair might not be fully prevented from sprouting. A new wart might grow where a previous one was removed.

That's why clients sign full-page consent forms, which discuss side effects and specify that the procedure may not work, before receiving service. It creates a clear understanding between the business and the clients. It also is an example of a concrete policy to protect the business in case a client complains later or resists payment.

Similarly, aestheticians treating skin at Jenna Starr's salon have clients sign waivers acknowledging they understand the risks of some of the treatments. For example, waxing to remove hair will pull off some skin. Other treatments can cause skin to break out in a rash.

At Starr's salon, the stylist specializing in hair extensions has clients sign a form acknowledging in writing that they understand they must maintain the extensions according to instructions.

Posted signs are other examples of concrete steps to protect a business. For instance, pointing to a sign that reads, "A $25 fee will be charged on all returned checks," or "24-hour advance notice required for canceling appointments" may be all you need to do to ward off clients who want to argue with your policies.

Signage can also work to emphasize rights a business already enjoys. A small sign at the front desk in Jenna Starr's salon and spa says, "We reserve the right to refuse service to anyone at our discretion." This right already exists, since the salon is private property and unwelcome guests who don't leave when asked are trespassing. Like the "No shirt, no shoes, no service" cards posted at the entrances of fast-food restaurants and other establishments that tend to draw the casually dressed, a "reserve-the-right-to-refuse" sign can foreshorten a negative encounter and send the problem individual packing. Of course, refusing service to people based solely on their skin color or other identities is not allowed and is not appropriate in our society. But within those identities are both good clients and bad clients. Your refusal of service will be based on the client's toxicity, a condition cutting across all segments of society.

The Toxic Client, as we have learned, is ubiquitous. With the rise of addictions and Entitlementia across the country their numbers are growing. They are most certainly headed your way, if they are not already your customers. You must be ready to know them and have the procedures in place to dismiss them.

A Toxic Client would find fault in paradise. They are that difficult and that unaware. Please be prepared for them.

Final Thoughts

"Experience is something I always think I have
until I get more of it."
~ Burton Hill

In business, as in life in general, "live and learn" is the healthiest and smartest approach to making sense of a trying experience, such as dealing with a Toxic Client.

A few old chestnuts speak to this truth:

"Burnt fingers are the best teachers."

"Fool me once, shame on you; fool me twice, shame on me."

"Experience gives us the shortcut after a long wandering."

You could probably come up with several more. The only benefit of encountering a Toxic Client is that you can learn how to avoid them in the future, and you will be strongly motivated to do so. You may carry the aftertaste of that experience for quite some time (indeed, perhaps for the remainder of your career). If so, savor it as a reminder.

Those of us who go into business for ourselves know there are risks involved. But we believe in ourselves, our work, and, yes, our clients. Our mission is to take care of their needs—to give value for the services or goods that we provide.

Our customers are gold to us. Without them, we cannot be in business. Happily, Toxic Clients are the exception, not the rule.

An unsatisfied client is not necessarily a toxic one. There may be valid reasons for a complaint or dispute. But we set our businesses up to resolve such problems and, whenever possible, send the customer out the door happy.

The reason Toxic Clients can be so venomous is that there seems to be no way to send them out the door happy. They seem to pose one problem after another. They divert us from helping our good clients. They challenge our professional skills and even, in extreme cases, our sense of self-worth.

The previous chapters have supplied you with strategies for coping with, and divesting yourself of, the difficult client. I hope that the horror stories shared here served to reassure you that you are not alone. You are not the only one who's suffered at the hands of a Toxic Client.

I, too, have endured such troubles, as you've seen. So have Matthew Martinez, Victor Lee, Gerald Westerbrook, Marvin Washington, Marla Welch, Scott McGee, Sandy Roth, Jenna Starr, and our other case history participants. Their names have been changed, and occasionally their names represent amalgams drawn from dozens of stories shared by real people. Even the experts whose words of advice were shared here— Kenji Sax, Frank Troppe, Lyn Millard, Mark Goodman, Tom Wheelwright and other entrepreneurs—are all real people in business who know about Toxic Clients because of their own real-life experiences. And they are still doing business, all the wiser for having dealt with Toxic Clients in the past.

The stories of Shirley, Pauly, Jeff Kerry, George Stinson, the Collingsworths, and all the other difficult customers are also drawn from real-life clients, despite their names or situations being changed. I hope that you have benefitted from their warning signs, and now have the wherewithal to begin to identify, dismiss, and avoid such clients from now on.

Active listening is a unique and very useful skill. You must learn to listen without distraction. You must learn to interpret and evaluate what is being said. When you are focused, you will learn to 'see' who is toxic.

You will come to know the Toxic Client. The client you don't like as a person, the one whose values you don't share, the complainer, the nitpicker and the no-payer.

You will know that they poison your workplace and divert your energies. They impact your good clients because with toxicity you are not able to perform at your top level for anyone. This knowledge is power. The power to break free of those who would drag you down.

Similarly, our country may be seen as being dragged down. There are voices deliberately seeking to divide us at a time when we surely need to be united. We can all start by being less toxic toward each other.

Reject the voices that lead to petty divisions.

I'd like to leave you with this final thought: Trust yourself. Trust your internal compass that guides you and helps you tell right from wrong. Chances are that each and every time you've encountered a Toxic Client (as we now see is very likely to have already happened), your instincts were giving you signals that something was wrong. Again, remember the German proverb that says: "Mistrust carries one much further than trust." If you feel that negative emotion, don't discount it. Use it to carry you beyond the Toxic Client.

Perhaps you were a novice and felt unsure of yourself in business dealings, so you dismissed the feeling. Perhaps you felt so desperate financially that you were willing to take any job that came your way.

Perhaps the client blinded you with promises of more work or referrals or money. But you probably knew, deep down, that something wasn't right. Don't ever ignore that feeling.

I encourage you to pay close attention to what your internal compass says, and resist the idea that "any job is a good job." When you become clear about the kind of clients you really want to attract, you may find that something almost magical happens: You'll be surrounded by the right kind of clients, and you will have all the work you can handle.

Good luck.

Appendices

We have included three appendices with information to help you collect from Toxic Clients.

Appendix A covers Mechanics' Liens which, while fairly specialized, are very useful for contractors and tradesmen. The help of a competent attorney is always recommended here.

Appendix B explains small claims court. You can appear in this court without a lawyer, informally plead your case and win. The court then allows for methods to collect what you are owed.

Appendix C deals with collection agencies. While you give up a percentage of what you are owed to the agency, you can at least collect something in most cases by using their services. A good agency saves your from wasting your valuable time trying to collect on old accounts.

Appendix A

Mechanics' Liens

Thomas Jefferson and James Madison are known for many American hallmarks, including the Declaration of Independence and the U.S. Constitution. For contractors and suppliers wanting to get paid they are also heralded as the fathers of mechanics' liens. To speed up construction of the new capital city of Washington the two Founders pushed for a strong lien law providing for payment. It may have been out of necessity: Who wanted to work for a government then (as now) without the money to settle up? A mechanism was needed to get the new city built, a unifying effort helping to thwart any British ideas of reconquest. (Of course, the British did burn down much of the city in the War of 1812, but that is a whole other story.)

Lien-like privileges already existed in France and Spain, and can be found as far back as the Roman Empire. But the American version, out of a national security necessity, offered more powerful rights to the land itself, as opposed to just the value of the improvements.

These liens also provide order. Without mechanics' liens a failed project could become an even greater mess. With no other way to get paid, to recoup your loss you and the plumber and the supplier of lumber would rush out to the project and remove all the plumbing and the wood and the improvements you made. Tearing down new construction is not a wise allocation of resources. Instead, each state mandates a formal procedure for a timely resolution and the balancing of claims between all contractors, suppliers and owners.

If you only collected 75% of what you were owed with your mechanics' lien that is better from a public policy standpoint than a new eye sore on Main Street that will never be rebuilt.

Mechanics' liens then are a useful tool for contractors and tradesmen providing labor and/or materials ("suppliers") to get paid and to give failed projects a running chance at new life. By creating a lien, a security interest against property, suppliers obtain a priority for payment if the property is sold.

Owners of real estate don't like to have mechanics' liens showing against their property. The lien says you don't pay your bills. Banks don't like to lend with such liens in place. But some people don't pay, which is why large construction companies have dedicated departments for the filing and enforcement of mechanics' liens. Follow their lead. The filing of a mechanics' lien is a good way to secure payment.

Although mechanics' liens vary considerably from state to state, and from lien to lien, they share certain common characteristics, including: (1) creation of the lien; (2) perfection of the lien; (3) defenses against the lien; and (4) enforcement of the lien.

1. Creation of Mechanics' Liens.
Mechanics' liens can be created on both real and personal property.

For example, as to real property, there can be construction liens, materialmen's liens, suppliers' liens, laborers' liens, and design professionals' liens.

With respect to personal property, there can be artisans' liens of all sorts, including liens for the storage, maintenance, keeping or repair of vehicles, mobile homes, manufactured homes, recreational vehicles, trailers, or aircraft; jewelers' and watchmakers' liens; liens for cleaning, pressing, glazing, or washing garments, clothing, wearing apparel, or household goods; liens on vessels; and liens on farm products.

This is by no means a comprehensive list of the types of mechanics' liens available. Indeed, the breadth of mechanics' liens varies considerably from state to state. Be sure to work with a knowledgeable local attorney on such matters.

Usually, a lien can only attach to the property of the person ordering the work. What if you are doing tenant improvements ("TI's") for a lessee in a large shopping mall? The lessee doesn't own the real estate. They only lease the space. You are one step removed from the lessor, the true owner of the real estate. There is great uncertainty as to whether a mechanics' lien for TI's attaches to the underlying real estate.

In a Massachusetts case, where the owner of the real estate consented to the TI's and was involved in the construction process, a lien could attach. Other cases go the other way. Again, a good attorney is needed to guide you through the process.

2. Perfection of Mechanics' Liens.

Before a mechanics' lien can be enforced, the lien first must be "perfected" against the property by taking the actions required under state law. Sometimes, the perfection of a mechanics' lien requires the lien claimant (the supplier) to file a lien statement against the property. This lien statement must include all required information, including a description of the property, the name of the present owner, and the amount of the lien

claim (the amount due for services rendered). This lien statement must then be filed in the proper registry (i.e. the county
recorder's office), within the amount of time provided by state
law. Lien statements must also, in most states, be provided to
owners of the property. This is especially important for subcontractors (such as an electrician doing work for a general
contractor). The owner may not know the scope of work a general contractor has committed the owner to pay, and so it is important for the subcontractors to provide such notice directly
to the owner.

Many states have a deadline for filing a lien after the work
is performed. For example, a 90-day state means that 90 days
after the last work is completed your lien must be in. But suppose on the 80th day you realize there is more original contract
work to be done. You go out to the job and perform the final
work. You now have another 90 days to file the lien. You have
just extended your deadline.

Priority is important when it comes to holding real estate
title.

Generally, claims against the property are prioritized by
the order in which they were filed. The difference between a
first deed of trust and second deed of trust is not the dollar
amount of the loan but rather when they were filed. The first
deed was filed first and has first dibs. Suppose a first deed se-
cures a $100,000 loan and a second deed secures a $200,000 loan
on the same property. At a foreclosure sale where the property
is sold for $150,000 the first deed holder gets $100,000, the second deed holder gets $50,000, and the owner gets nothing. The
second deed holder just lost $150,000. Priority is important.

There are some exceptions to the first-to-file rules. Tax liens
jump ahead of prior claims. This makes sense. The government

is always going to structure it so it gets paid first. Mechanics' liens can also jump ahead of the other earlier filed claims. If your state's liens are "inchoate" (pronounced *in-ko-ate*) they relate back to when the work was performed not when the lien was filed. As long as it is later perfected by properly filing, the lien holder gains a priority advantage.

Again, this varies from state to state. Pennsylvania liens are inchoate, whereas Maryland's are not. In Maryland, when the property is sold or goes through bankruptcy the lien rights may be extinguished if there is not enough money to go around.

To further complicate things, in some states a construction loan takes priority over a mechanics' lien. If you do business in several states you may need a separate attorney for each state since the laws can be so different.

Once perfected, the supplier's lien claim is secured by the property. For example, if the lien is for $10,000 and the property is sold, in most cases, and with some wrinkles discussed ahead, the first $10,000 out of escrow goes to the supplier. As is evident, a lien is a good way to get paid.

In some cases, once perfected, a mechanics' lien against the property will prevent the property owner from selling the property without first obtaining a lien release from the supplier. Again, the supplier will be paid.

3. Defenses Against Mechanics' Liens.

Property owners can assert defenses. One of the most common counter arguments is that the lien was not perfected properly. An owner may assert that the lien statement was not filed within the time period allotted by state law, or that the lien claimant did not follow the very narrow pathway to perfect the lien. Because mechanics' liens are governed by strict procedural rules, these arguments are frequently successful.

Another common defense is that the lien is invalid because the supplier knowingly demanded too much money for the storage, repair, maintenance, or other services to the property. This defense may be anticipated when the property owner already has disputed the amount of money demanded. Only claim what you can support and what is reasonable.

As well, the work must qualify as that which goes directly to the improvement of the property. Owners will argue that the work being liened does not constitute an improvement. For example, a construction fence, while necessary during a build-out, is not going to become a permanent part of the realty. Such a cost is not allowed to be secured by a mechanics' lien.

4. Enforcement of Mechanics' Liens.

Rather than simply waiting for the property to be sold, a mechanics' lien claimant is entitled to commence a foreclosure proceeding in order to get paid. There usually is a time period—which again varies considerably from state to state and from lien to lien—within which a supplier can commence a foreclosure proceeding against the property. As an example, your state may have a 90-day limit from the date the work was last performed to file the lien and then a one-year limit to foreclose on the property to satisfy the lien. In some states, if the foreclosure is not timely, the supplier will not be able to enforce a lien claim against the property. Thus, although the supplier still may be owed money, the amount of the lien claim no longer will be secured by the property.

If the supplier is successful in foreclosing upon the property, then the court basically will order the property to be sold by the local sheriff's office at a public sale or auction to the highest bidder. If the property is sold to a bidder for more than the amount of the lien claim, then the net proceeds of the sale or auction will be disbursed first to pay any tax liens and then next to the supplier to pay the amount of the lien claim. The remainder of the net proceeds will be disbursed to any secondary secured parties (such as a bank holding a first and/or second deed of trust) and if anything is left then to the property owner. You can thus see why banks don't like to see a mechanics' lien against a property they have loaned on. Such a lien upsets their priority for payment.

Suppose the owner has skipped town and there are twenty lien holders and two banks fighting over what is left. Some cases will go to court, which can get quite expensive and time consuming. You will have to prove you did your work in a timely manner according to the contract and without defects. You run the risk that others will question your efforts and appeal any decision to the next court up. This case could go on for years. In other cases, prudence may prevail. Attorney's fees are not recoverable in mechanics' lien litigation and savvy players recognize that sharing of the loss without throwing more good money after bad is the best way to proceed. Instead of spending the time, negative energy and money to go to court only to get a 30% recovery, perhaps it is best for all parties to settle now and get a 60% recovery.

Each case will be different. But without filing the lien you aren't even in the payment discussions. File your liens so you have priority.

CONCLUSION

Perfecting and successfully enforcing mechanics' liens can be somewhat difficult. They can also be remarkably effective.

Since each state has its own specific rules and requirements for mechanics' liens, be sure to work with a local attorney familiar with your state's laws. Together, you can use these powerful liens to get yourself paid.

Appendix B

Small Claims Court

Small claims courts are one of the most overlooked and underutilized litigation tools for the solution of many common legal problems. They provide an excellent opportunity for a non-lawyer to present his or her case for resolution to an independent third party. Unlike other courts, which can be formal and daunting, and which generally require the retention of an expensive attorney, the small claims courts usually are informal, and they often (but not always) prohibit lawyers from participating.

However, before describing the general procedures in small claims courts, a word of caution is in order. Small claims cases do not in any way represent "free money." You definitely will "earn" your money in small claims court. If you win in small claims court, you then next have to collect your money, which we will discuss.

Litigation, even in a small claims setting, is a time-consuming proposition, and you always should treat litigation as a last resort. Sometimes, it may seem as if you have no other way forward. But know that you do have other options. Alternative dispute resolution, including mediation and arbitration, often can save people time, money and relationships.

One of the constants of litigation is that the outcome is uncertain.

People considering litigation usually believe (rightly or wrongly) that they have "a good case". However, litigation is an adversarial process and, almost by definition, one side eventually must "lose." So, at the end of the day, it would appear that one-half of all litigants are "wrong," because they did not really have "a good case" after all.

That said, if you provided goods and services to someone and were not paid, in the absence of bad behavior on your part, you will have a good case. Why not get paid?

GENERAL PROCEDURE IN SMALL CLAIMS COURTS

Every state (and some local courts) have their own rules for small claims court. Those rules do change. Which is why this discussion is general in nature. After reading it your job is to find out the rules both in your state and your local area. The clerks are usually very nice and helpful about providing this information if you are nice and cordial to them when asking the questions.

You should be aware that small claims courts are courts of "limited jurisdiction," that is small claims courts have very strict limits imposed upon them by state legislatures as to what they can and cannot do. This is particularly true with respect to monetary damage limits.

If you are thinking about filing a small claims court case, the first thing you should do is to check the monetary damage limits of your small claims court. You can learn by simply calling the court clerk and asking what the dollar limit is. Some courts have a $5,000 limit, others a $10,000 limit or more. You must know the amount ahead of time.

If you are owed $6,000 and the limit is $5,000 in most courts you can sue for $5,000 and just give up the other $1,000. Check ahead if this is allowed in your area. If you want the full $6,000 you may have to hire an attorney to pursue a claim in a higher level court.

Once you know you fall within the court's dollar limit, then filing your case in small claims court generally involves the following four-step procedure: (1) suing someone; (2) going to court; (3) collecting your judgment; and (4) appealing, if necessary.

1. Suing Someone.

There basically are six elements involved in suing someone in small claims court: (a) writing a demand letter; (b) naming the defendant; (c) choosing the right court; (d) filling out the court forms; (e) filing your claim; and (f) serving your claim.

a. Writing a Demand Letter.

Some (but not all) small claims courts require that you formally ask the other side for payment before you go to court. (This relieves the court's work load by not having to hear easily settled cases.) If you do not know how to write a formal demand letter, then you easily can find help online in the form of sample demand letters. Basically, you set out the facts and demand that you be paid within, for example, 10 days. The letter does not have to be very long, but rather clear enough to set forth your demand.

b. Naming the Defendant.

This sounds really easy, but it sometimes can be incredibly difficult to find the EXACT name of the person or company you are suing (the defendant).

(i) Naming an Individual as Defendant.

If you are suing an individual person, then you should write that person's first name, middle initial (if known), and last name. If the person has used different names in the past, then you should write each different name (or alias) as an "aka" (also known as). For example, "John D. Doe, aka Richard R. Roe, Defendant."

(ii) Naming a Husband and Wife as Defendants.

If you are suing a husband and wife, then you should write both of their full names. For example, "John J. Starr and Brenda B. Starr, Defendants."

(iii) Naming a Sole Proprietorship as Defendant.

If you are suing a sole proprietorship, i.e., a business owned by one person, then you should write the owner's name and the business's name. For example, "John J. Starr, dba (doing business as) Quadcopters, Defendant."

(iv) Naming a Partnership as Defendant.

If you are suing a partnership, then you should write the names of the partners individually, followed by the name of the partnership. For example, "John J. Starr and Mary M. Morton, individually and dba Starr & Morton, and Starr & Morton, a partnership, Defendants."

(v) Naming a Corporation as Defendant.

If you are suing a corporation, then you should write the exact legal name of the corporation. For example, "Quadcopters, Inc." If, for any reason, you do not know the exact legal name of the corporation you are suing, then you may be able to do what is called an online "Business Entity Search" with the office of the Secretary of State in the state where you live, in order to find out the exact legal name of the corporation you are suing. Note the entity's registered agent and address. You will be able to serve the lawsuit at that address.

(vi) Naming a Limited Liability Company as Defendant.

If you are suing a limited liability company, then you should write the exact legal name of the limited liability company. For example, "Quadcopters, LLC." Again if, you don't know the exact legal name, go onto the Secretary of State's website to see if they are organized as an LLC. If an LLC or corporation is not current on their state filings you can still sue (and may have a piercing the corporate veil argument to obtain a claim against the individuals).

(vii) Naming a Business Owned by a Corporation as Defendant.

If you are suing a business owned by a corporation, then you should write the corporation, followed by the dba of the corporation. For example, "Quadcopters, Inc., dba Up, Up, and Away."

c. Choosing the Right Court.

There is usually a small claims court in every county in the state, so it is important for you to choose the right court to file your claim. If you file your claim in the wrong county, then the court may dismiss your claim, and you will have to re-file your claim in the correct county. Worse yet, if you have waited until the last minute to file your claim, and the time to file your claim has run out, then you may end up losing your case.

The general "rule of thumb" is that you should file your claim in the court where the defendant either lives or does business. However, there are some exceptions to this rule. If you are not certain where to file your claim, then you might be able to contact your small claims court's legal adviser or self-help center for assistance.

(i) Contract.

If you are suing because of a contract, then you also may be able to file your claim in the county where you signed the contract, in the county where the contract was broken, or in the county where the contract was to be performed.

(ii) Purchases.

If you are suing because you bought something or paid for a service, then you also may be able to file your claim in the county where you now live, in the county where you lived when you bought or paid for the item or service, or in the county where the item or service was bought or paid for.

(iii) Credit Cards.

If you are suing your credit card company, then you also may be able to file your claim where you now live, where you lived when the contract/application for the credit card was signed, or where you signed the contract/application with the credit card company.

d. Filling out the Court Forms.

In order to file your claim, you will need to fill out the small claims court forms, including the proper form for filing a plaintiff's claim. You should ask your local court clerk if there are local forms you need to fill out. In addition, some small claims courts also have online forms that you can fill out on their websites. If you are not certain which forms you will need to fill out, then you may (or may not) be able to contact your small claims court's legal adviser or self-help center for assistance. In addition, you may (or may not) be able to ask your small claims court's legal adviser or self-help center to review your paperwork before you file it.

e. Filing Your Claim.

After you have completed filling out your court forms, then you must give your forms to the clerk of the small claims court, in order to file your claim. Naturally, you will have to pay a fee to the clerk, in order to file your paperwork with the small claims court. The amount of your fee generally will depend upon how much you are suing for. If you cannot afford to pay the filing fee, then you sometimes can get a fee waiver, so that you do not have to pay the filing fee.

After you give your forms to the clerk of the small claims court, the clerk will look at your forms, and may even ask you a few questions. The clerk generally will keep the original of the forms for the small claims court, and will give you a copy for yourself, as well as other copies for each of the defendants you are suing.

At this time, the clerk generally will give you a court date for your court hearing. You should be extremely careful to mark your calendar with the date of your court hearing. It is critical that you attend your court hearing on time. If you do not attend your court hearing on time, then the judge probably will dismiss your case or make a decision without hearing your side of the story. In addition, if the defendant has filed a counterclaim (sued you back), and you do not attend your scheduled court hearing, then the court will not consider your position, and you may well lose on the defendant's counterclaim, as well.

f. Serving Your Claim.

Once you file your claim, then you will need to serve your claim on the defendant(s), in order to alert the other side about the lawsuit. "Service" generally is when someone else (not you or anyone else listed in your complaint) gives a copy of your court paperwork to the person, business, or entity you are suing. Service is designed to let the other side know that they are being sued; what you are asking for; when and where the trial will be, and what they can do about it.

Service is very important. You may (or may not) be able to contact your small claims court's legal adviser or self-help center for assistance. Some small claims courts will direct you to the local sheriff's department. For a small fee a sheriff will go out and serve the defendant. I like this procedure. Sometimes just the gravity of a sheriff showing up can lead to a settlement.

If the local sheriff doesn't provide this service there are local process servers who will. The key is that whoever does the serving must get back to the court showing that the defendant was notified. If you don't receive a copy of the service, you should follow up with the court to make sure they received the notice of service. It wouldn't hurt to follow up in any case.

2. Going to Court.

As previously noted, it is critical that you attend your court hearing on time. Better yet, go ahead of time.

I always tell my clients that if they can spare the time they should go watch the court in session a few days before their hearing. If they can't get away they should at least go an hour before their case is called. As well, if you are just starting out in business and don't have a claim but do have the time, consider stopping into your local small claims court. You will be better prepared, enlightened and even entertained.

The importance of an advance screening is to see how the system flows. How are people dressed? (I always suggest wearing nice clothes as a sign of respect to the court. In a close case it may be the deciding factor, so give yourself an edge.) What arguments work with the judge? Does he or she want just the facts? Or is it better to tell more of a story? Is the judge not listening to and/or cutting off emotional arguments? Then don't make such arguments. You will learn a great deal as an interested spectator.

Please know that each judge has their own style. Some are gruff, others have a light touch. Many are all business. If possible, watch the judge who will handle your case. But also know that your judge may not be assigned to the case until the morning of the hearing.

When your case is called, you should be fully prepared. You will explain to the judge the facts of the case, why you are filing your claim and exactly what action you want the court to take, or, what you want the court to order the other side to do.

Plan in advance what you are going to say at your trial. Practice in front of a mirror. Ask your family for constructive criticism. Try and make it a fun exercise.

Decide what the main points of your case are, and you should be certain to take proofs of these points with you to your trial. If the action involves a contract bring several copies with you. Give a copy to the judge, if he or she doesn't already have one. Point to the key provisions (for example, Paragraph 8, Payment for Services) so as to make it easy for the judge to get to the heart of the matter.

Only provide the most necessary documents to prove your point.

The court will not be receiving volumes of documents for a $5,000 case. Try to anticipate what the other side is going to say and how you will answer them when they do. As well, step into the other side's shoes. What would you say if you were them?

You should take any lay witnesses with you to your trial. "Lay witnesses" are witnesses who saw or heard what happened in your case. In addition, you should take any expert witnesses with you to your trial. "Expert witnesses" are witnesses with specialized knowledge, who may be able to assist the court on technical issues that might arise during the trial. When you need them to speak, you will politely ask the judge if you can call your first witness. Lay the foundation for their testimony by asking them questions. What is their name? Are they aware of the case? What is their testimony as to it? While it is all very informal you still want your case to have a logical flow to it.

If you need documents that you do not have, then it may be possible for you to subpoena these documents by filling out a small claims court subpoena well in advance of your trial. Likewise, if you need a witness to attend your trial, and that witness cannot or will not attend your trial, then you also may be able to fill out a small claims court subpoena, requiring the witness to attend. Know that if they don't want to attend the may be hostile to your case and may actually hurt it. Ask yourself: Can I prove the case without their testimony?

Finally, it may be important that you research your case prior to your trial. If your case is simply one for a collection of monies you are probably fine. But if your case involves interpretations of laws and regulations, you may want to do some online research. You may want to go to your county's law library, in order to learn the substantive law that applies to your case. This way, you will understand better what the judge is trying to say to you at the time of your trial.

3. Collecting Your Judgment.

Even if you are successful in winning a judgment against the defendant, you still must collect your judgment. In some cases a defendant will have no assets, in which case your judgment may be worthless. (Of course, you still have the satisfaction of prevailing over the deadbeat, money collected or not. That at least has some value.)

Still, you probably should prudently ask yourself: "Is it worth my time to go after someone I will never collect a dime from?" Or, in other words: "Will the time and money it takes to go to small claims court be worth the likely outcome?" If you do not ask yourself these questions at the start you may find yourself in a bigger hole, in terms of time and expense, at the finish. Then again, if it is your first time in small claims court and you are doing it for the experience, does it really matter if you don't collect? With the right attitude and a long term view, probably not. Go for it.

Even though the court will not directly collect your money for you, they will issue the orders and other documents you will need to collect your money from the debtor (the defendant who now owes you money.) Make sure you give the debtor an address where he or she can mail you the money. If the debtor does not pay you by the date ordered by the court, then you should write to the debtor, and include a copy of the court order. You also should remind the debtor that, if they don't pay you, that penalties and interest may start to accrue. Let them know you will take all the necessary legal action to collect your money.

Some courts have unique and effective procedures you can use for collection. You may want to ask the clerk what remedies for collection they offer before you even file the case. For example, if the debtor runs a brick and mortar business, in some counties you can have a sheriff go out during a busy time and "tap the till". The officer stands by the cash register and takes the money that would have otherwise gone to the debtor. This is very embarrassing for the business owner, and certainly not a good customer experience, and can lead to a prompt payment of monies owed.

Other courts will allow you to attach monies in a bank account. How do you find out where they bank? If you haven't written a check to them (whereby the key information will be on the back of the canceled check) you can go back to court and ask where they do their banking. Of course, this will give them a heads up that you may try and attach their account. In which case, they may switch bank accounts before you can attach the now old account.

A trick for doing this without attracting attention has worked for a number of clients. Wait for a month or so after you have won in small claims court. By that time, many people have moved on and even forgotten about the judgement. Have a friend go into their business and write a check for a small amount of goods and services. If the debtor does their business out of town have your friend call in a phone order. Make sure their checking account is one that returns canceled checks or at least provides legible copies. When your friend's canceled check is retuned you will have the information needed to attach the account. Try to estimate when the most money is in the account. Is it at the end of the month, before the accounts payable go out after the first? If so, put the court order in at that time. Know that if you are owed $5,000 and you only get $3,000 from their checking account you can always try again for the rest you are owed.

If you are still not collecting you may want to try a collection agency. They will take a healthy percentage of what you are owed, but at least you'll get something. Know that many debtors will cry poor and claim they have nothing anywhere for payment. A good collection firm can pierce through such stories, many of which are not true.

4. Appeals.

If you lose your small claims court case, you may under some local rules have a right to appeal the decision to a higher court. Generally speaking, only the defendant can file an appeal of a small claims court judgment.

However, if the defendant counter-sued you by filing a counterclaim, then you can appeal.

Again, depending upon the local rules, you may be entitled either to a completely new trial—a so-called trial de novo (or new trial) on the merits of your case, both factual and legal—or to an appeal on the factual record that you have established before the small claims court—a so-called trial de novo (or new trial) on the record only.

In the former case, where an appeal consists of a trial de novo on the merits, you will have a completely new trial, and you will be required to present your case all over again "from scratch." However, because this trial de novo will not be held in small claims court, the parties will be permitted to hire attorneys to represent them during the trial de novo in the higher court.

In the latter case, where an appeal consists of a trial de novo on the record only, it is essential that you establish a good factual record before the small claims court, because, generally speaking, and with few exceptions, you will not have an opportunity to present any new evidence to the higher court on appeal. Furthermore, the higher court hearing your small claims court case on appeal will be entitled to accept as true all factual evidence contained in the record on appeal that is supported by "any substantial evidence". You should be aware that the "any substantial evidence" standard is a relatively easy standard to meet.

If an appeal is filed against you, you may want to seek the counsel of an attorney. You may be entering a more formal area where an attorney is needed.

CONCLUSION

If you cannot work things out informally with the person or business you are thinking about suing, and if you truly believe that litigation is necessary and that there is no other alternative, then you would do well to heed Davy Crockett's motto: "Be always sure that you are right, and then go ahead!"

Appendix C

Collection Agencies

Debt collection agencies can be useful in collecting money from Toxic Clients. There are about 4,000 debt collection agencies in the United States, and they average about a 20 to 30 percent recovery rate on bad debts. Still, in most years they return $50 billion to business owners.

Why Use a Debt Collection Agency?

Debt collection agencies often are able to collect bad debts when small business owners are unable to do so. Once debt becomes overdue, debt collection agencies have a definite advantage over small business owners. Collection agencies are more persistent and assertive than small business owners. They are in the business to get paid.

Debt collection involves sending out numerous letters and making numerous telephone calls, all of which can be very time-consuming for small business owners. By using a collection agency, small business owners are able to free up a great deal of time, which then allows them to pursue their chosen businesses, rather than debt collection activities. A collection agency has many advanced tools that small businesses owners simply do not have, which will allow them to locate and communicate with debtors.

Collection agencies can also report debt against the credit report of the business owing money. Whether the debt is paid or not, a collection record can remain on the credit report for 7 years from the last 180 day late payment. Any business that cares about building business credit will not want such a report on their record.

When to Use a Debt Collection Agency?

Business owners should consider using a debt collection agency when a customer debt is three months (90 days) overdue. However, many business owners are using collection agencies even earlier, especially in situations where the owner has already sent out some letters and made some telephone calls without any response from the debtor, or where the debtor has passed a bad check. The longer you wait in such cases, the less likely you are to get paid.

How Much Do Collection Agencies Generally Charge?

Debt collection agencies typically work on a contingency fee basis, meaning they charge the business owner a collection fee only if they are successful in collecting a bad debt. Their fee is contingent upon collection. Depending upon the type and amount of the debt involved, collection agencies will keep anywhere between 10 and 50 percent of the total collected. If the fee is 25% of what is collected and the agency collects $200 on a $500 debt they keep $50 (or 25% of the $200, not the $500). Know that the contingency fee can be negotiable. If the amount is large attempt to get a lower rate. There are many agencies to choose from so feel free to shop around and compare fees. Don't be afraid to counter a higher rate with a lower one.

How Do Debt Collection Agencies Work?

A. Traditional Third-Party Collection Agencies.

Third-party collection agencies are the traditional debt collection agencies. They receive bad debts from small business owners and then send out letters and make telephone calls to debtors. Initially, they send out a first letter to the debtor. If they do not receive a response to their first letter within about one week, then they start making daily telephone calls to the debtor and sending more letters to the debtor. The purpose of these letters and telephone calls is to persuade the debtor to pay the bill right away, or else to get the debtor to schedule some sort of payment plan. Again, the more time that goes by the lesser chance of collection.

Failure to collect means the agency is not compensated for their time. Put in this context and you can understand why some debt collectors come across as mean and nasty. They have heard every excuse in the book from Toxic Clients and just want to get paid!

B. Non-Traditional First-Party Collection Agencies.

In today's economic climate, there are an increasing number of non-traditional first-party debt collection agencies. They are called first party because they quietly take over the debt collection operations of small businesses. As such, a debt owed to XYZ Plumbing appears to be collected by XYZ's staff. But the job has really been outsourced to ABC Collection. Some debtors are put off by being sent to collection and this strategy removes the sting of it, while freeing up XYZ from actually having to do the collections. Like traditional agencies, the non-traditional agencies must still follow all the state and federal rules.

What Can Collection Agencies Not Do?

Under the federal Fair Debt Collection Practices Act (FDCPA), collection agencies (which do not include creditors attempting to collect their own debts) must tell debtors, in their first communication, that they are attempting to collect a debt and that any information obtained will be used for that purpose.

In addition, collection agencies generally are prohibited from engaging in certain activities, including, but not limited to, the following:

(1) calling debtors repeatedly or contacting them at unreasonable hours (before 8:00 a.m. or after 9:00 p.m.); (2) placing telephone calls to debtors without identifying themselves as debt collectors; (3) contacting debtors at work if their employers prohibit it; (4) using obscene or profane language; (5) using, or threatening to use, violence; (6) claiming debtors owe more than they do; (7) claiming to be attorneys if they're not; (8) claiming that debtors will be imprisoned or their property will be seized; (9) sending papers that resemble legal documents; (10) adding unauthorized interest, fees, or charges; and (11) contacting third parties, other than debtors' attorneys, credit reporting bureaus, or debtors' original creditors, except for the limited purpose of finding information about debtors' whereabouts.

Some Useful Tips in Hiring A Collection Agency

There are many different collection agencies available for businesses to hire. Know that some collection agencies specialize in working with large businesses, whereas others prefer smaller accounts. Before hiring any collection agency, make sure it is a good fit for your business.

Before hiring anyone, you should always: (1) inquire whether the collection agency has "skip tracking" capability (this is important because some debtors have been known to "skip town"); (2) check to be sure the collection agency is licensed, bonded, and insured; (3) make certain the debt collection agency adheres to the rules of the FDCPA; and (4) compare the contingency fee of the debt collection agency with the contingency fees offered by other debt collection agencies. Shop around.

When looking for an agency ask for referrals from your attorney, accountant or other business people you trust. You can also search ACA (Association of Credit and Collections Professionals) International for a member agency in your area.

Consider checking any agency's report with the Better Business Bureau. A few complaints will be normal (they are in the business of demanding money) but a very large number of complaints could represent a very large red flag.

Conclusion

Be ready, quick and persistent. When you realize you will have a problem collecting get the debt over to the agency. The sooner they are involved the more likely you are to collect something (less the contingency fee.) Waiting 120 days or more to pursue collection significantly reduces your chance of seeing anything. Have a collection agency pre-selected and ready to collect before you ever need it.

About the Author

Garrett Sutton, Esq. is a nationally acclaimed corporate attorney and asset protection expert, who has sold more than 850,000 books guiding entrepreneurs and investors. Garrett's best sellers include: *Start Your Own Corporation, Run Your Own Corporation, The ABCs of Getting Out of Debt, Writing Winning Business Plans, Buying*  *& Selling a Business* and *Loopholes of Real Estate* in Robert Kiyosaki's Rich Dad Advisor series. He is also the author of *How to Use Limited Liability Companies & Limited Partnerships* and the co-author of *Finance Your Own Business*. Garrett enjoys helping entrepreneurs to succeed. He has more than thirty years of experience in assisting individuals and businesses determine their appropriate corporate structures, limit their liability, protect their assets and achieve their goals. Garrett is the founder of Corporate Direct and Sutton Law Center, which since 1988 have provided affordable asset protection and corporate formation and maintenance services. His articles and quotes have been published in *The Wall Street Journal*, *New York Times*, CBS.com, Time.com and Credit.com. More information is found at www.CorporateDirect.com and www.sutlaw.com.